FROM WARWICKSHIRE

Edited by Simon Harwin

First published in Great Britain in 2000 by
YOUNG WRITERS
Remus House,
Coltsfoot Drive,
Woodston,
Peterborough, PE2 9JX
Telephone (01733) 890066

All Rights Reserved

Copyright Contributors 1999

HB ISBN 0 75431 765 X
SB ISBN 0 75431 766 8

FOREWORD

This year, the Young Writers' Future Voices competition proudly presents a showcase of the best poetic talent from over 42,000 up-and-coming writers nationwide.

Successful in continuing our aim of promoting writing and creativity in children, our regional anthologies give a vivid insight into the thoughts, emotions and experiences of today's younger generation, displaying their inventive writing in its originality.

The thought, effort, imagination and hard work put into each poem impressed us all and again the task of editing proved challenging due to the quality of entries received, but was nevertheless enjoyable. We hope you are as pleased as we are with the final selection and that you continue to enjoy *Future Voices From Warwickshire* for many years to come.

Contents

Holly Jones	1
Debra Lapworth	2

Avon Valley School

Jenny Carter	2
Kate Johnson	3
Michael Pails	3
Andrea Howe	4
Ellie Postles	4
Christopher Boddy	5
Faye Davies-Lowde	5
Louise Miller	6
James Daymond	6
Laura Barnes	7
Daniel Jones	7
William Goodman	8
Lewis Watson	8
Lucy Carter	9
Jonathan Wilkinson	10

Alderman Smith School

Elly Wilson	10

George Eliot School

Amy Garnham	12
Sophie Caul	12
Daniel Wright	13
Lisa Rogerson	14
Chris Oliver	14

Hartshill School

Katie Little	15
Clare Harris	15
Clare Davenport	16
Jenna Martin	16
Benjamin Banks	17

Adam Green	17
Andrew Quick	18
Naomi Carter	18
Andrew Cross	19
Jodie Dewis	19
Ede Roche	20
Claire Jacques	21
Sarah Corbett	21
Katharine Stait	22
Claire Grzeszczyk	22
Ben Turner & Adrian Talbot	23
Adam Skyner	23
Kirsty McCaffery	24
Dane Cooper	24
Amy Vaughan	25
Andrew Male	25
Clare Ellard	26
Jade Moore	26
Amy Kelly	27
Andrew Webb	28
Rebecca Martin	28
Ed Fulker	29
Rachel Wood	30
Andrew Sullivan	30
Lisa Morris & Emily Arkinstall	31
Andrew Louden	31
Danielle Cope	32
Alex Croxall	32
Liz Webster	33
Andrew Gordon	34
Shaun Wilson	35
Kelly Greenaway	36
Mark Burton	36
Gemma Saddler	37
James Dunne	37
Natalie Whitehouse	38
Katherine Hayes-Smith	38
Nichola Smith	39

Rebecca Elliott	39
Victoria Smith	40
Vicki Prince	40
Ryan Tyler	41
Samantha Wilson	41
Jamie Robinson	42
Hannah Mills	42
Melissa Franklin-Weeks	43
Ben Korpan	43
Robert Finch	44
Tara Moore	44
Kayleigh Marie Urquhart	45
Joanne Lunney	46
Sarah Ward	46
Greg Shearing	47
Nicola Randle	47
Jamie Everard	48
Natalie Smith	48
Kylie Sheridan	49
Jonathan Brock	49
Scott Holland	50
Andrew Meads	50
Kayleigh McCaffery	51
Andrew West	51
Duane Beers	52
Michelle Whitmore	52
Leanne Reed	53
Adam Cramp	53
Lesley Mara	54
Líesl Hill	54
Lisa-Marie Cope	55
Simon Canning	56
Shaun Galletly	56
Chris Ballard	57
Victoria Hatcher	57
Joel Burke	58
Leanne Hodgson	58
Kate Marshall	59

Nicola Brown	60
Rachael Pickard	60
Kristi Jane Rogers	61
Simon Hayllar	61
Rebecca Bennett	62
Hayley Wilson	62
Adam Nicholls	63
Richard Moore	64
Adam Hartshorn	64
Mark Roach	65
Terri Pratt	65
Sammi Smith	66
Louisa Mitchell	67
Laura Duggins	68
Wesley Green	68
James Stewart	69

Kenilworth School

Gemma Burke	69
Alison Gregory	70
Clare Haley	71
Luke Hollingworth	72
William Mack	72
Melanie Taylor	73
Clare Webster	74

North Leamington School

Ben Spann	75
Gavin Ranson	75
Emma Mortimer	76
Quentin Oury	76
Sophie Huckvale	77
Sybella Davis	77
Chris Halfpenny	78
Sam Hargraves	78
Emma Metcalfe	79
Jonny Ayres	79
Nathan Batchelor	80

Samuel Hayler	80
Amy Tucker	81
Rachael Chesworth	82
James White	82
Tracey Talbot	83
Jamie Williams	83
Sabrina Savariar	84
Andrew Ward	85
Jackie Perry	85
Harriet Whitehead	86
Laura Wilkins	86
Mary Addyman	87
Alice Griffin	88
Ian Garrett	88
Nisha Rai	89
Kathryn Riley	90
Katie Travis	91
Richard Evans	91
Miranda Forth	92
Kohinoor Meghji	93

St Benedict's RC High School, Alcester

Alistair McLeod	93
Hazel Truscott	94
Stephen Capron	94
Charlotte Richards	95
Michael Gurrie	96
Joel Brimmell	96
Jenny Miller	97
Jimmy Marino	98
David Whittaker	99
Callum McCormick	100
Helen Boffey	100
Luisa Petta	101
George Godding	102
Katherine Millward	102
Katherine Mann	103
Lewis Williams	104

Anne Gould-Fellows	105
Mimi Fisher	106
Rachael Jones	107
Ian Burnip	108
Daniel Houston	108
Sam La Vedrine	109
John Partridge	110
Vicky Bostock	110
Gemma Ludlow	111
Sophie Cooter	112
Peter Doubtfire	112
Alenka Lamare	113
Helen Flynn	114
Roberto Frascona	115

Stratford-Upon-Avon High School

Hayley Hartis	115
Ceri Slade	116
Peter Middleton	117
Nicola Sach	117
Laura Cox	118
Sarah Hicks	118
Carly Hanks	119
Louise Welsh	120
Sophie Parslow	120
Lily Anstey	121
Ella Selwood	122
Lee Stewart Coldicott	122
Hazel Ingram	123
Jessica Eastgate	124
Amber Compton	124
Nicola Sach	125
Sarah Morris	126
Claire Hampstead	126
Sandy Chan	127
Lucy Selwood	128
Tiffany Holman	129
Katie Strugnell	130

Cara Morgan	130
James Breen	131
Sarah Scowcroft	132
Caroline Maisey	132
Emma Johnson	133
Hannah Ulyatt	134
Kerry Oakes	135
Daniel Simpson	136
Simon McCoy	137
Oliver Bigland	138
Anna Turton	139
Stuart Taylor	140
Sarah Fernott	141
Zoë Smith	141
James Righton	142
Marcus Lemberger	143
Anna Sanders	144
Lisa Fernandes	145
Tom Fidler	146
Rebecca Caden	147
Keira Wilson	148
Rebecca Young	149
Grace McAteer	150

The Poems

CHRISTMAS DAY

Christmastime,
fun in the snow.
All the presents
wrapped with a bow.
Rudolf the reindeer
leading Santa's sleigh.
As they go along
they're eating all his hay.
We hang up our stockings
ready for Christmas Day.
When it finally comes
we all shout 'Hooray!'
Christmas Day arrives,
all the children come down
and dive into all their gifts,
tearing them away with their mitts.
As the day comes to an end
all the parents send
their children off to bed,
clutching their new teds.
And say,
'What a wonderful day.'

Holly Jones (16)

FIRE CIRCLE

Life stealer,
As hot as the sun,
Circling around you,
With no way out.

Earth burner,
As bright as a star,
Bursting up high,
Killing environment in its path.

Debra Lapworth (12)

VIRTUAL REALITY

V irtual reality will be a thing of the future
I   f everybody had it then that would be really cool
R eality check, it has been around for ages
T oday you could go virtual car racing or virtual skiing
U nder the helmet you are transported to
A nother world, where everything is virtual reality
L ike I said before it will still be a thing of the future.

R eality has always been around with us but this is the virtual version
E ven if you don't get it you could still go to the
A rcades to play on the car racing or the motorbike racing machines
L iving in a virtual reality world, now I know
I   know that there is no reality
T oday you can be transported to another world
Y ou might just enjoy.

Jenny Carter (13)
Avon Valley School

PEACE MAKES THE WORLD GO ROUND

Peace makes the world go round
and makes people get along.
You watch the ambulance go by
and you more than likely
know the cause.
Ambulances
rush to wherever they're needed.
Then you hear the families crying
while the nurse tells them they will
never see their son or daughter again.
Soon you will start having to look over
your shoulder and be alert
wherever you go.
So what is going to happen
to the future voices?

Kate Johnson (12)
Avon Valley School

FUTURE VOICES

Future voices in the air.
Unusual sounds everywhere.
Talking tellies, talking trains.
Business people use Virgin trains.
Robotic sounds moments away.
Aliens will invade and take us away.
They will play our games and eat our food.
Peace to war but for some people it's a chore.

Michael Pails (12)
Avon Valley School

FUTURE VOICES

Tape recorders, TVs and
talking cookers all
hope to be voices
in the future.
Strangers in our class
becoming famous,
animals learning to
communicate with
each other.
Aliens coming down
to Earth and eating
us all.
What are the world's
Future voices coming to?

Andrea Howe (12)
Avon Valley School

FUTURE VOICES

In the future we might hear
Animals talking loud and clear,
Cookers talking, governors walking,
Aliens connecting, tax men collecting.
Robotic sounds all around,
Children falling to the ground,
Adults talking, teachers mourning,
Doctors calling, nurses bawling.
In the future we might hear
Robotic sounds very near,
Radios blasting, computers crashing,
Aliens landing, labour commanding.

Ellie Postles (12)
Avon Valley School

Virtual Reality

V eterans tell their stories of wars
I n cybernetic worlds,
R ay guns and death rays are used throughout these wars,
T hen people realise what the future will hold,
U tter destruction or utter peace,
A lly with alien races or
L ive on countless odyssey for a new fresh start.

R obotic androids scatter the world,
E volution kills off the world,
A ndroids now think for themselves,
L ittle aliens become discovered,
I n the future people rely on robots,
T ill the sun explodes,
Y ou have heard this warning.
Beware.

Christopher Boddy (12)
Avon Valley School

Future Voices

Future voices everywhere,
giving advice
and helping out.
She's going, we're losing her,
give her more oxygen now.
Pulse is slowing down, we're all steady.
Yes my first time saving a life.
I wonder what my future is holding for me,
and what will my future job be?

Faye Davies-Lowde (12)
Avon Valley School

FUTURE VOICES

F uture boss is seen as Mr Ross
U p at the crack of dawn, as short as a prawn
T aking the pain he's heading for fame
U ndercover he's living with his brother
R acing around he's spending the pound
E nding in shame he's taking the blame.

V ery quick it makes me sick
O ld and bold he says, 'Just do as you're told.'
I ll and underpaid, yet not displayed
C hildren screaming as their smile is beaming
E verlasting Mr Ross is now just the big, bad boss.

Louise Miller (13)
Avon Valley School

THE FUTURE

F uture voices like robots and little baby tots
U nknown voices from far out places
T remulous voices from frightened faces
U nnecessary violence and screaming lots
R ugby lions roar
E specially when the other team score.

V irtual reality fills people's heads
O utsiders plead to get in
I ndoors there is such a din
C hildren crying for their beds
E arth cringes from alien faces
S ilent voices from far and away places.

James Daymond (13)
Avon Valley School

FUTURE VOICES

In the year 2000
There will be little aliens
Jumping, hopping around
Keyboards tapping
Laser guns zapping
There will be aliens
Jumping, hopping around.
People talking
Doors slamming
Aliens singing
Bosses shouting.
Aliens will be still there
Mammals howling
People talking
Little green aliens
Coming from Jupiter.

Laura Barnes (13)
Avon Valley School

FUTURE VOICES

One day aliens will land on our Earth,
Learn how to play football,
Learn how to surf.
Their heads will be completely bald,
Their skin scaly and cold.
Their face a lime green,
Their intellect supreme.
They will be so great
I will have an alien for my mate.

Daniel Jones (12)
Avon Valley School

FUTURE VOICES

Future voices coming near,
You can hear them loud and clear.
Tape recorders, TVs too,
They are all here for you.
Virtual games for us to play,
Every hour of the day.
Aliens walking here and there,
Oh, no what a *scare!*
Robots helping here and there,
You must be aware,
Because they will strike,
Anyhow, anywhere.

So be aware!

William Goodman (12)
Avon Valley School

FUTURE VOICES

Robots and aliens communicating with us,
Talking objects like computers and cookers.
Us becoming parents,
Better education for our children.
Peace at last in the virtual world just moments away.
Talking pets is unbelievable.
Our world has been taken over by monkeys.
Robots doing all our work.
Everyone with a great, big smirk!

Lewis Watson (12)
Avon Valley School

SHUT UP!

Shut up, *oh* do shut up,
turn that music down,
my mum goes on and on with a frown.

Shut, *oh* do shut up,
turn that music down,
on and on my mother goes with a great, big frown.

In my bedroom crashing round,
hear my music go pound, pound, pound.
Lucy, Lucy turn that down
don't you even make a sound.

My mum's a fusspot, quiet's her name,
give me music to keep me sane.
Quiet's needed for old fuddie duddies
or whatever they're called.
Quiet's a boring game, no fun in it at all.

At school we're told to be quiet,
Oh not here as well.
Quiet's for the library so whisper if you can,
being told to be quiet is such a bore,
I can't wait till the weekend when it's quiet no more.

Lucy Carter (12)
Avon Valley School

FUTURE VOICES
*(Dedicated to Great-Grandfather
Sir Robert Thomas, aged 98 years)*

When I'm old I wonder how I'll sound.
I'll probably be very quiet,
as quiet as a mouse.
I could be very loud,
louder than ever.
I could be silent or not speak at all.
I could speak with more meaning or not mean
anything at all.
I could speak slang or maybe with quality.
I could speak with love or hate but whatever, I
know it will be too late,
I know that my voice will never be the same again.

*Jonathan Wilkinson (13)
Avon Valley School*

THE ROOM!

I went walking in the streets,
saw a room with a light on . . .
Are you wondering what I see?

There's a girl in the corner
with a hollow brow
and a guy with a smile
which is kinda like a frown.

There's a fella smoking,
that's worrying all the time . . .
And the corner of his heart's gone black
from the guy with the cigarettes who is
trying to write a song . . .

The girl who looks out of the window
is dreaming all day, of how it could be
and knowing of how it could be.

While Bob Marley plays on in the moody
background.
If you think about it
the world's like that room.
Different kinds of people
with different moods
but in ways they're all the same.

Don't forget the rock dudes
sitting round the stereo,
and the hippie in the centre of the room
practising yoga whilst drinking milk.
And the girl who loves America
who would rather be there than here.

As Bob Marley plays on in the moody
background.

If you think about it
the world's like that room.
Different kinds of people
with different moods
but in ways they're all the same.

Don't forget,
Remember we're all the same.

Elly Wilson (15)
Alderman Smith School

Future Voices

All around me I hear the words
Of a million different voices.
A small child being lured
By his mother with a bag of sweets.
There's two people I see every week,
They find something to talk about
Every time they meet.
And there's a lady
As old as the winds of time,
She never even utters a word or line.
It goes to show, everyone's different.
A newborn baby cannot speak,
Although it grows every week.
We can be nasty, hurtful, kind, helpful,
It's we who make the choices.
But it's we who are the world's
New future voices.

Amy Garnham (13)
George Eliot School

Future Voices

When will our world be finished?
Will it be gone soon?
What's going to happen?
Will we have three moons?

Will we *all* get killed,
Or maybe just a few?
Is it gonna explode
Or expand and turn us blue?

Will there be such a thing
As 2000 and one?
Or is that it,
We will all be gone?

Sophie Caul (13)
George Eliot School

SAVE THE ENVIRONMENT

'Save the world just for a year!
Because Mother Nature is having such a tear.'
'Oh shut up I'm the litter bug.'
'That's it I'm pulling the plug.'

We will use all the electricity up,
All so we can have tea for a cup.
All over the world we cut down trees!
All so we can say, 'Miss more paper, please!'

'I've never seen so much rubbish;
From sweets and drinks to make us *'tubbish'*.'
'In half-term I'm going to Blackpool;
I hope I don't have to call it *Tackpool*!'

Every week we use lots of carbon-fused tar,
All so we can lay roads for fuel-consuming cars!
So save the world just for a year,
Because . . . Mother Nature is shedding a great, big tear.

Daniel Wright (11)
George Eliot School

Millennium Poem

Millennium is coming like a rocket into the sky
The future is whispering along
Big Ben ticks at 12 midnight as we start to see
                         the millennium light
Who knows what it's all about?
New inventions everywhere
Everyone is getting prepared for the fun and the joy.
The clock strikes 12
People will be singing, dancing, partying all night long
Welcoming people to the millennium
The new year of joy.

Lisa Rogerson (14)
George Eliot School

Future Voices

The future voices of this land are dying,
While injecting themselves, the
parents with heroin, they think not of
the child but of the high, the buzz, the rush.
They think of the latest buzzes on the
street, heroin, dope, coke, spliff.
They care not for the child but for
the high, the rush, the buzz.
This is why,
for the buzz!

Chris Oliver (13)
George Eliot School

SILENCE

Quiet.
Like the silence of a moonlit graveyard,
shadowed by the trees.
Like the stealthy feet of a thief.
Like a deserted school as a breeze blows
brown leaves round the empty playground.
Like the hush of a funeral parade as it moves
its mournful way along.
Like the lack of words as lovers watch a
beautiful sunset together.
Like a dead telephone wire which no
longer communicates.
Like the ominous silence before a storm.
Like the quiet of thought as you read this poem.
Like me.

Katie Little (11)
Hartshill School

THE SNOWSTORM

We were stuck in the middle of a snowstorm,
The cat was miaowing at the door,
It was as cold as ice,
And as hard as bullets,
And it was getting colder by the minute.
Suddenly the sun came out,
It was like a light bulb,
As bright as day,
But as dark as night
And the storm was starting to *stop!*

Clare Harris (12)
Hartshill School

ENERGETIC

Energetic,
Like the cheetah that runs as fast as the wind.
Talkative,
Like chatting birds.
This is how people see me,
But am I?
I can be quiet as a mouse,
That doesn't last very long.
I can be helpful by tidying my room
But it still ends up messy.
I can be angry
But will you ever see?
Maybe not,
Maybe you will,
May you won't . . .

Clare Davenport (11)
Hartshill School

HALLOWE'EN

H allowe'en is spooky
A ll night long
L anterns in the dark
L ighting up the park
O h but it was scary
W hen witches come out to play at night
E erie evening and spooky nights
E very child loves to trick or treat
N othing but ghosts, ghouls and goblins
    come out to play on Hallowe'en night.

Jenna Martin (12)
Hartshill School

BLACKPOOL

B lackpool, a favourite holiday for me
E xciting entertainment for everybody
N ever a dull moment when I am there
J olly shop keepers they certainly care
A ction, bright lights, rides galore
M any happy days and even more
I ndescribable happiness
N ow the only thing that's missing is the monster from Loch Ness.

B atches, hot dogs fresh and new
A nd American soda and Slush Puppies too
N othing can beat paddling in the sea
K icking at the waves as they come at me
S treaks of lightning light up the sky as I drive away and say goodbye!

Benjamin Banks (11)
Hartshill School

HALLOWE'EN

H allowe'en - it's great fun to scare people
A ll that night it's always quiet
L aughter is all we hear
L ots of children screaming with fright
O range pumpkins glowing up
W itches fly on brown broomsticks
E ggs thrown at windows
E very Hallowe'en night
N ight breaks down and witches are no longer in the sky.

Adam Green (12)
Hartshill School

WHAT DO PEOPLE THINK OF ME?

My name is Andrew Quick,
It is.
My mates call me thick,
I'm not!
My parents think I'm crazy,
Me!
But my teachers think I'm lazy,
Never!
My brother thinks I'm strange,
He can talk!
He really wants me to change,
Tough!
My nan thinks I'm really sweet,
True! True!
More than you can say about my
smelly feet,
Phew!
My sister thinks I'm totally mad,
What can I say?
I just like a laugh, she should be glad,
She's not glad about anything.

I'm none of these things, I'm just me
and what you get is what you see.

Andrew Quick (11)
Hartshill School

MATT

I have a new baby cousin called Matt,
He has green eyes and massive ears,
But when he cries he's a lousy little toad.

Naomi Carter (12)
Hartshill School

HALLOWE'EN

W hen the nights start to draw, out come the witches
I n the light of the moon we see the witches casting spells on the little children
T he children, one by one they turn into vampires
C reepy it may seem but wait until they come to you
H ow can we escape it?
C an you think of a way to destroy the witches?
R aces these are like
A nd we will win every one
F ight we shall
T orture is what we'll give but we'll take none at all.

Andrew Cross (13)
Hartshill School

ARMY ANTS

We are the army ants,
we go wherever we want.

If anybody gets in our way
we will eat you for our lunch.

We may be little
but we still are strong.

We are small, red figures
and we are never wrong.

We are wild and free
in the jungle happy as can be.

Jodie Dewis (11)
Hartshill School

HARTSHILL'S ANCESTORS

Many thousands of years ago
Prehistoric man came to visit.
He saw the rocks, running water
And said 'It's not too bad here, is it?'

He made his home hereabouts
With woolly mammoths aplenty.
With all that food running around
His belly was never empty.

His relations weren't too far behind,
Growing crops and rearing animals.
Then the Romans came bringing their
Roads, pottery and a lovely line in sandals.

Boudicca wanted to be in charge
But the Romans wouldn't let her.
She said, 'Let's sort this out man-to-man,
I'll see you in Mancetter.'

Her army was made up of locals,
They were really quite a shower.
But unfortunately she lost the battle,
So much for 'girl power'!

Now thousands of years on in '99
If you visit Hartshill Hayes
The only battle cry you'll hear
Is 'Have you paid and displayed?'

Ede Roche (11)
Hartshill School

THE BASEMENT

The basement is scary and dusty
Nobody ever dares to go down there
Somebody cried for help that night
As the man heard a roar of a bear.

Then the next night
The man once again heard the bear
He walked to the basement
And saw something strange
And the man fainted in pain.

The girl that cried for help
Never got out of the basement
She was lost in there
For years and years.

Claire Jacques (12)
Hartshill School

SARAH CORBETT

S illy, stupid, spectacular and sweet
A lways hiding under my sheet
R acing, facing my challenger's bet
A lways at home cuddling my pet
H elping my mum do the jobs.

C ounting the seconds when my brother sobs
O rders flying about my head
R ight at home in my bed
B eating up my brother who I hate
E very night I come in late
T aking a walk is very good
T aking a walk through the mud.

Sarah Corbett (11)
Hartshill School

Do You Remember?

The bombs fell like rain
The bombs felt like rain
But I felt them a lot, lot more
As they crashed on the floor
We were very, very lucky
That they didn't hit one of us
But then one hit a house
Do you remember?
Screaming came from every direction
Crying, as well
I just couldn't take it anymore
My whole family wasn't
The bombs went 'bang'
The buildings went 'crash'
And then it was all over in a flash.
Do you remember?
Everything went quiet
And all that was lying there
Were bodies of children everywhere
Do you remember?

Katharine Stait (13)
Hartshill School

The Phenomenal Witch

The phenomenal witch spreads her witchcraft.
The phenomenal witch hangs over the world
like a spider in a web.
Like a demon, cruel, horrible, wicked and don't
forget ugly.
The phenomenal witch dies with hunger.

Claire Grzeszczyk (11)
Hartshill School

THERE IS AN OLD LADY WHO LIVES IN A TREE

There is an old lady who lives in a tree
If you don't believe me just come and see.
Look high up in the sky,
Look high up in the trees,
There she is looking down from the trees.
I told you so
Then all of a sudden
She pours a bucket of cold water on me.
And that's the tale of the old lady that lives in a tree.

Ben Turner & Adrian Talbot (12)
Hartshill School

MY POEM

My name is Adam Skyner,
I am really, really cool.
I live with my mum and dad
and I'm definitely not a fool.
I have two sisters and a brother
and one very fine dog
called Vicky and when she's hungry
she eats like a hog!
I have a cockatiel called Popeye
and another one called Pat,
a hamster and a rabbit
and a big, brown rat.
I like football, gym and tennis,
and swimming a lot as well.
My mum thinks I'm a menace
and I suppose she can tell.

Adam Skyner (11)
Hartshill School

MY POEM

On holiday I was at Panda's Palace,
All of a sudden I felt so embarrassed.
I kicked a punchbag,
And all I done
Was nag my mum.
'I've bruised my toe.
I've bruised my toe.'
My mum replied 'It looks so sore,
Do I have to put up with this anymore?'
'I hate it here
I hate it here.'
The beach was horrible
And it was cold.
It was a night
For a good night's sleep.
My sleep was so, so deep.
The next day we had to travel
A long, long, way home.

Kirsty McCaffery (11)
Hartshill School

ME AND CHRIS

Me and Chris are like ninjas really smart and stealthy.
Me and Chris are like rich men really cool and wealthy.
Me and Chris are like cheetahs running through the plain.
Me and Chris are crazy, people say insane.
Me and Chris are like football stars flying down the wing.
Me and Chris are Cantanas honoured like a king.
Me and Chris are pop stars soaring to number one.
Me and Chris dream on.

Dane Cooper (11)
Hartshill School

WITCHES' BREAKFAST

'Come, come you young witches, it's
breakfast time for you.'
'What's for breakfast, head of all witches?'
'Fried slug with a splash of bat's blood'
'And to drink, head of all witches?'
'You lot have got bog water.'

'Ha, ha, ha, all witches must sing the witches' song.'
Here we are sitting on the broomsticks,
Waiting for our food,
'Yum, yum,
Here it comes,
Yum, yum,
Yum.'

'Eat, eat, your witches' breakfast is served.'

Amy Vaughan (12)
Hartshill School

TONY HAWKS

T urning with a 180° kick flip
O nto the grind pole
N ose grinding all the way
Y urning into a 360° rocket air

H e goes into a 180° Madonna
A nd lands a 360° method
W alks into a Japanese tail grab
K nocking his opponents flat
S ailing into a special 900°.

Andrew Male (12)
Hartshill School

TRICK OR TREAT

Children go round on Hallowe'en,
Having fun trying not to be seen,
They knock on doors to get some sweets
But before that they say 'Trick or treat?'

Some are skeletons, some are witches,
Some are monsters with nails through their heads,
Some are vampires with teeth instead,
Carrying pumpkins full of sweets,
Some kids think it's very neat!

But one important thing to remember,
Hallowe'en is always in October,
Having fun all night long,
Until the clock struck twelve with a *dong*,
The pumpkin glowing with a candle inside,
Makes you think about your face,
Eating cakes, sweets and chocolates,
I think it's neat because of the sweets!

Clare Ellard (12)
Hartshill School

THE PIED PIPER '99

I'm in the Hinckley pantomime
I'm lovin' every minute.
It's better than the Nuneaton one -
And there's not a mobcap in it.

I do a rat dance and even
Wear a wig,
The only disappointment is I
Miss the cowboy jig.

They even have a magician,
Who does a real neat trick -
My grandma doesn't get it -
I think maybe she's thick.

The dame he makes us laugh and laugh
You should see the way he's dressed-ed!
If he walked down the street like that,
He would probably get arrested.

Jade Moore (12)
Hartshill School

WILL NEVER BE . . .

Last night I was walking along the seaweeded shore,
The sound was great, the waves gave a roar.
The moon shone brightly upon my weary soul,
Waves lapping over roll after roll.
The sun shone a reflection, a silvery green,
Off the seabed which gave out a gleam.

Oh the sand felt great through my toes,
There was still a sandcastle, which gave out a pose.
I strolled along the beach for years it seems,
Carefully I rested my tired head and hoped for sweet dreams.
There I lay staring at the stars,
Looking out for Neptune or even Mars.

A sudden light blew up the sky,
Oh I wish that I could fly to a distant land,
Hold a star in my hand,
As far as I and life can see,
My true hopes and dreams will never be.

Amy Kelly (13)
Hartshill School

The Pirate Ship Sick Poem

In 1996 me and my cousins went to Blackpool
It was only for the day but we said 'Cool!'
After parking the minibus,
My uncle replied 'We must be here by dusk.'
We went to Blackpool Tower,
But the wind was full of power
We couldn't go to the top
So on Level 4 in a jungle gym we had a drink of pop.

From there we went to the piers,
On Central Pier my auntie bought my dad a pair of furry ears!
Then it was the South Pier,
There was a ride that made me feel quite queer.

Then it was Blackpool Pleasure Beach,
There was a ride which had a caterpillar going through a peach.
It was then the pirate ship,
And I felt sick!

It was then dusk
So we went back to the minibus.
That night I thought of a crypt,
It was a 'pirate ship'.

Andrew Webb (11)
Hartshill School

Flanders Field

In Flanders Field,
The soldiers lie,
In Flanders Field,
The soldiers die.

In Flanders Field,
Is peace and war.
In Flanders Field
For evermore.

Rebecca Martin (13)
Hartshill School

IN ENGLISH, ABOUT ENGLISH

A poem is always in English
But never about English
And I think that's cruel
To use English in such a manner.

Like Keats, Blake and company
All wrote about flowers and trees
But never about the dictionary
That fulfils their needs of poetry.

So all budding poets who want to rhyme
Listen to what I say
English will get you all in good time
Or rhymes will soon be away.

Cos you'll strive and you'll stretch
To rhyme words together
But they'll all be gone and nothing will rhyme
And your poems will be such a crime.

So every now and again when you wish
For inspiration passed to you on a dish
Write about plain old English
And it will rhyme just like this . . . poem.

Ed Fulker (13)
Hartshill School

DOWN AT THE ZOO

D own at the zoo
O n a very cold day
W here the kids are playing
N ear the lake.

A nd at 12 o'clock when the food comes out
T he lions cry with hunger.

T he children cried when they saw a fly
H ands were empty
E very day at 7 o'clock the zoo always opens.

Z ed the elephant always goes
O ooooh
O ooooh.

Rachel Wood (12)
Hartshill School

THE GOLF HOLE

The ball flies through
The air and lands on
The light fluffy grass - bang!
The ball is flying through
The wind - tink!
It hits the firm
flag
and
drops
in
the
wide
hole.

Andrew Sullivan (12)
Hartshill School

THAT'S LIFE!

Why, why does it have to be me,
The one that always gets hurt,
Life just isn't fair,
Just because I'm different,
Why does it have to be this way?
But that's life!

What is life?
What is the meaning of it?
Is it meant to be cruel?
Why are we born?
Why do we die?
What's the point of me being here,
Living in this hell?
But, I suppose that's life!

Lisa Morris (14) & Emily Arkinstall (13)
Hartshill School

I WISH I NEVER DONE IT

I've just set it up
It's going to go with a mighty bang.
I wish I never done it,
But they made me.
If the police found out they'd kill me
I feel sick, sick as a dog for doing it.
Think of the families and children
They're so innocent.
Why does it have to happen to them?
I wish I never done it.

Andrew Louden (13)
Hartshill School

BULLYING

Some friends are kind, some friends are bad,
Some friends will comfort you when you are sad,
Others will laugh and point and stare,
And then they will follow you everywhere.

They chase me home and pull me down,
And beat me till I'm black and brown,
They kick, they punch, they make me bleed,
'Help . . . somebody! I'm in need.'

I'm lying there on the ground,
Crying in pain, I look around,
I'm being bullied, I'm letting them do it,
I'm going to show them, I'll beat them to it.

I'm going to stand up, really I am,
I'm not going to take it, I'll show them I can,
But . . . who's there to help me? No one I see,
I have no friends, they all bully me.

Danielle Cope (13)
Hartshill School

TEACHERS

Teachers, teachers, I'm going mad,
They send you bonkers and make you sad.

I admit I was going mad,
But sage advice then came from Dad.

'If you shut up and stop concerning,
You'll have some fun and start your learning.'

I thought about my dad's advice,
He has the brain of small woodlice.

So I said to Morris and Sidaway,
'There's something wrong but I can't say.'

They couldn't help so I gave up,
So I had a drink and smashed my cup.

Alex Croxall (13)
Hartshill School

DRUGS

Drugs are bad
They make you go mad.
There's cocaine, tobacco,
cannabis, heroin, dope and coke.
There is also cake.

Medicine and tablets
are also drugs if you have too many.
Alcohol is a drug and so is coke
if you have too much.
Drugs can be found in anything.

Drugs are happening every day
all around the world.
Tobacco and cocaine
can cause tar in your lungs.

Lung cancer is when the lungs
have tar in them, making it
harder to breathe.

Liz Webster (13)
Hartshill School

SCHOOL DINNERS

It's after 12.00 and your belly starts to ache,
The bell finally goes, that's all you could take,
You stare into the lunch hall,
And the queues are never small.

You decide to join the massive queue,
And cringe when you've seen the lunchtime menu,
Awful things and mouldy chips,
The things that you'd see in a skip.

Finally you reach the front,
The lady stares at you, then grunts,
The lady's face covered in moles,
She says to you 'Try our sausage rolls!

Or how about a burger that's flat
And cold baked beans to go with that?'
'Please, no!' you cry, you're rather hasty,
'Please give me something that's half tasty!'

You've told your friends about this story,
All the bits, both good and gory,
Now your friends are in stitches,
Don't you wish you'd brought sandwiches?

Andrew Gordon (13)
Hartshill School

SCHOOL

School is that place, that horrible place,
What a useless waste of space.

The horrible place that isn't good,
Teachers demand your sweat and blood.

Oh my God, it's after 8am,
Better hurry or I'll be late.

Who invented this dungeon zone,
The place where children ache and groan?

The three old ones, Maths, English, Science,
They might as well have a torture licence.

Maths, oh no, I've got it today,
I ain't done my homework, so I'll say

My dog ate it, had a lovely meal,
Or, it was ripped to bits by a 10ft seal.

English, oh no, I cannot mention,
Forget the homework and it's *detention!*

Science is bad, a whole lot worse,
I can't fit it into one measly verse.

Two more years, and I'm away,
Two more years I wouldn't stay.

Shaun Wilson (13)
Hartshill School

DEATH!
(A fictional poem)

Dead! She fell to the floor!
Her lips were blue, she moved no more.

The sparkle that was always in her eyes,
Gone! The dark clouds filled the skies.

It hit me like an arrow through my heart,
She'd gone away, into the stars.

I needed her, for good times and bad,
She was good to me, when I lost my dad!

But now she has gone forever,
I'll miss her and won't forget her.

The tears won't stop for a long, long time,
My mum was precious, her memories are mine!

Kelly Greenaway (13)
Hartshill School

MARK BURTON

M otor cars I really like
A stras, Porsches, are really fine
R evving up my motor cars
K a's really take me down

B eeping horns make my day
U ltra steering is so ace
R over cars are so cool
T ime myself around the track
O ut and about in my best car
N ow that's the end of my cool song.

Mark Burton (11)
Hartshill School

SLEEPING ROUGH

Freezing cold, soaking wet, with nowhere to go.
Looking at the passers-by, I see no one I know.
I look to my right and see a doorway.
I think this is where I'll stay.
I drop my things and settle down
On the hard and rocky ground.
As I try to get to sleep,
I hear the heavy sound of feet.
'Oi mate, you're in my space,'
A voice comes from a dark face.
I slowly rise to my feet,
I hear my heart begin to beat.
I move away, it's really tough,
When you're sleeping rough.

Gemma Saddler (13)
Hartshill School

MY SIMILE POEM

J ackass I can be,
A dventure I can see,
M ad is me,
E ncouragement I lack
S elfishness I attack

D urable is my brain,
U ndermine my sister is my game,
N otion ideas I come up with,
N ecessity for model cars I have,
E erie is my sister.

James Dunne (11)
Hartshill School

HORSES

Horses are playing,
On a cold day
Rain was coming,
Soon I have to ride
Even though he is naughty,
Shows are coming soon.

In the box it was scary,
Naughty horses are falling.

A fun day,

Finally we are back,
In a warm stable
Even though it was warm,
Lying down in a field
Down by the river.

Natalie Whitehouse (12)
Hartshill School

THAT'S ME!

My eyes are as blue as the ocean,
My hair is as blonde as the golden sand,
My singing is as good as Celine Dion,
And I dance like a daffodil in the spring.
I'm as friendly as the autumn breeze,
As warm-hearted as the comforting sun,
As cuddly as a kitten,
And as busy as a bee.
As playful as a puppy,
And as cheerful as a clown can be.
That's me!

Katherine Hayes-Smith (11)
Hartshill School

MY POEM

The play was here,
I was really nervous.
I got ready in the changing room.
My dress was too long.
It was like a wedding dress.
I went on the stage, legs like jelly.
The dance I was in, went fine.
I started to walk off,
Oh no!
I slipped over my dress
And I fell.
My stomach felt like I had skydived.
I felt so embarrassed.
I felt like everyone was laughing at me.
I was going red.
The audience didn't even seem to notice!

Nichola Smith (12)
Hartshill School

DOGS

Dogs come large to small,
Fat to thin,
And come when you call.
It's a pity
That they chase my kitty.
They're just sweet and funny
Like a jar of honey.

Rebecca Elliott (12)
Hartshill School

The Journey

Driving in the car with Mum,
a sicky feeling in my tum,
we've driven so far my bum's gone numb,
when will we arrive?

Driving in the car with Dad,
trying not to be so bad,
a holiday, of that I'm glad,
when will we arrive?

Driving in the car again,
watching wipers in the rain,
my little brother's being a pain,
when will we arrive?

Now the car is slowing down,
driving through a seaside town,
Mum and Dad have lost their frown,
I think we have arrived!

Victoria Smith (11)
Hartshill School

The Toucan

The toucan is a tropical bird
Always seen and always heard.
The toucan has a tropical coloured beak
They bash them up the trees
This is how the toucans speak.
The toucans favourite food is grapes
They sit in trees and laugh at apes.

Vicki Prince (11)
Hartshill School

HAIR AS BRIGHT AS GOLD

My hair is as bright as gold,
Even a lion isn't as bold,
As Ryan Tyler, hard as nails,
One day I'll go off the rails.

Like a nutcase in a cell,
I'm as loud as a chiming bell.
Without a care I'll speak my views,
Like a reporter, on the news.

My parents think I'm as bad as the devil,
But I say 'I'm on the level!'
I've tried as hard as God to write this poem,
As he did to get the river flowin'.

I'll act like Tom Cruise to complete my mission,
Which is to win this poetry competition.

Ryan Tyler (11)
Hartshill School

WHY?

Why did it have to happen to me?
What did I do?
Who planted the bomb?
Who killed my family?
I'm all alone.
Someone please *help me*
I have nowhere to go.
It was about one year ago now.
What did they have against us?
I will say it again
Please help me!

Samantha Wilson (13)
Hartshill School

IRA

Bang! Bang! Bang!
Here come the bombers
Bang! Bang! Bang!
Here Come the men
Bang! Bang! Bang!
We're going to kill al ten men
Bang! Bang! Bang!
We're the best army in the world
Bang! Bang! Bang!
Get out of the way
Before I shoot you
We will be good.
I will burn your home down.
Bang! Bang! Bang!

Jamie Robinson (13)
Hartshill School

ACROSTIC POEM

H ave you been to Guides?
A fter school on Tuesdays
N ow you can join because you are ten,
N early every week we do activities,
A ll the time we have fun,
H ave you been to Brownies?

M aybe you could start
I have been, it's great,
L ove it when you go,
L ittle ones go to Rainbows,
S ame time next week?

Hannah Mills (11)
Hartshill School

THE WAR OF IRELAND

Night falls and the war is on
People are screaming, guns are shooting.
I am so scared inside.
So cold with blood dripping down my body.
I feel like ice, as if I can't move.
I wonder what will happen.
My life is in ruins,
It's all such a mess.

Bombs are dropping all around me.
I can't find my family.
I am so scared, so lonely.
My life is in ruins, it's all such a mess.
I wish this would all go away.

Melissa Franklin-Weeks (14)
Hartshill School

THE BOMB

I am an IRA bomber
I hide the bomb in a bin next to a police station
Then I walked off down a dark alley
I heard someone coming behind me
So I hid behind some boxes and stayed quiet
It's the police I thought, but it wasn't . . .
It was a tramp and he was out of his head
He wouldn't cause any trouble so I got out the detonator
I could hardly feel my fingers because they were cold as ice
I flicked a switch to arm the bomb
Then counted to 10 . . . flicked the switch
Bang!

Ben Korpan (13)
Hartshill School

ME!

I was the sort of person that people picked on.
I am the sort of person that makes people laugh.
I'm also the sort of person that gets frightened
when I get lost.
When people get to know me, they get to like me.
How do people see me?
Do they see me as old or young?
Do they see me as smart or scruffy?
People shouldn't judge others by their looks,
but their personality.
Only I can decide my future.
What will I do when I grow up?
How will I do in my exams, will I get A's, B's or C's?
Questions?
Questions?
Questions?
It's all up to me!
But that's the least of my worries.
I've got enough to think about,
Now I'm in Hartshill!
But I'll do well . . .
What better school could you ask for!

Robert Finch (11)
Hartshill School

BIG BANG!

As I walked through the dark cold alley,
I was thinking what to do, how to do it?
My mind went like a time machine,
My heart felt like it was going to explode.
The bomb was black as coal,
My hands were shaking as I put down the bomb.

I started to set the timer.
I thought to myself why am I doing this?
I'm not a murderer.

The timer was set for twenty seconds, then I walked off.
As I started to run faster and faster I heard a really *big bang!*
Then I knew I was a murderer.

Tara Moore (13)
Hartshill School

KAYLEIGH MARIE URQUHART

K elly, Jamie, Moretz, Lenax,
A re the cousins that I've seen and know,
Y et there's many many more.
L aura B and Laura F
E nemies are they
I am happy, I am cheerful, I am
G entle and kind. Oh no
H elp! There's my brother

M any likes,
A nd dislikes,
R umbling through my mind.
I dislike doing homework and dislike
E nglish too.

U sually I'm
R eading, but if not, I'm
Q uarrelling with my brother
U nless I'm asleep
H obbies, I've got millions
A t least I've kept a few,
R eading is one of my hobbies, my favourite authors,
T he teacher, she's the best.

Kayleigh Marie Urquhart (11)
Hartshill School

Problem Child!

My little sister is a problem child
She races round the house
Acting really wild.

My mum gets really mad
When she screams and shouts
I've never known anyone so bad.

I would love to have a normal sister,
Because when I take her out
She behaves like a sore blister.

What can I do to make her behave?
Wait, I have an idea
I could try to lock her in a cave.

She's so wild that stupid
               problem child!

Joanne Lunney (12)
Hartshill School

The Storm

The rain was sharp like glass,
Lightning was bright as the sun,
Thunder so loud as a drum,
Wind like a dog that howls,
In the night and cold like ice,
The hail was stones pounding down on my window . . .

It's over, it's over.

Sarah Ward (12)
Hartshill School

A Poem About My Funniest Moment

I was in Skegness, in a sports shop,
Buying a new Aston Villa top.
I walked out the shop, and stood there in pride,
Then ran to the beach and sat by the tide.
The beach was deserted, and I was alone,
Eating my chocolate ice-cream cone.
I ran across the beach, then started to sprint,
Now eating an Aero Mint.
Then suddenly my trousers fell down,
You know what I felt, I felt like a clown!

Greg Shearing (11)
Hartshill School

The Keys

We went on holiday,
To stay for a week,
But when we got there,
We had to go to sleep.

I left my key on my bed,
Then I shut the door and went red,
I had left my key on the bed.
And then I ran out of the building,
And started to hide.

I slipped over by the slide,
My mum and dad found me in the end,
And just say they went round the bend.

Nicola Randle (11)
Hartshill School

Bang, Bang, Boom, Boom!

Bang! Bang! Boom! Boom!
Another bomb has hit,
Bang! Bang! Boom! Boom!
Hundreds die and get hurt,
Bang! Bang! Boom! Boom!
Families get split up,
Bang! Bang! Boom! Boom!
I'm not going to cry,
The IRA give us doom,
Bang! Bang! Boom! Boom!
Another bomb will hit soon,
Bang! Bang! Boom! Boom!
I hope I don't die soon,
Bang! Bang! Boom! Boom!
I hate the IRA.

James Everard (13)
Hartshill School

The Bomb And I

I planted a bomb.
It was like a tennis ball.
When I set it for 40 seconds I was scared, I was nearly crying.
I had to run, run like the wind.
Then I got to the base and heard a great big *bang*.
I ran back to see, there was about 2000 people dead.
I felt horrible and I never did it again.

Natalie Smith (13)
Hartshill School

OH NO!

Embarrassing, embarrassing
When I was in year five at my old school,
I was sitting in the classroom
with my legs crossed.
I was waving my hand up in the air,
'Miss I need to go to the toilet,'
In the end she let me go.
I came back out and everyone was lining up,
I went into the hall, everyone was staring at me,
Then all of a sudden, a group was laughing at me.
When we came out of the hall, I felt a bit uncomfortable
I hid behind my mate's coat.
She said 'Get off or you're heading for a punch.'
I knew she was only joking.
I ran into the toilet and pulled up my skirt.
I'm glad it was Friday.

Kylie Sheridan (11)
Hartshill School

WAR IN FLAMES

As the bomb was dropped all was silent.
Many people were wiped out like trees in a bush fire.
The sky was as black as oil.
Children shed tears like raindrops down a window.
Buildings fell down as the fire grew.
Families were separated as the storms began to come.
People began to lose hope.
People fell down like lemmings off a cliff.
People ran to and fro but it was no use.
The actions of this war were cruel and evil!

Jonathan Brock (13)
Hartshill School

THE SILENCE IN THE AIR

The street was quiet that tragic day
The sky was clear
The town was crowded with shoppers
The silence was broken by a deafening bang and darkness
I could feel a heavy weight on my legs and dust was everywhere.
The street went quiet for what felt like forever
Then there was voices and people screaming
I could hear the sirens of the emergency crew
It seemed like forever until I heard a voice ask me if I was OK.
Then I felt the weight lift from my legs and I was carried away.

Scott Holland (13)
Hartshill School

WILL THIS EVER STOP?

This beautiful country has just gone black,
Because the IRA are back.
One after another,
Another terrorist attack.
One after another,
The IRA are back.
Everywhere goes dark again,
People look out of the window,
Scared in case they get hurt.
People pray,
Will it ever stop?
By the looks of things,
It will never stop.

Andrew Meads (13)
Hartshill School

THE RHYTHM OF CLICK-CLICK

You can hear screams from miles around
as the IRA are gunning Protestants down.
There was a girl, skipping, alone in the street.
Not realising how fatal her next few minutes could be.
Children are lifeless on the floor.
Their screams are like thunder
Crying for help
But no one is there, no one.
The rhythm of click-click is faint, almost silent.
But I know they are there.
The soldiers, the IRA, the murderers.
I hear one behind me but as I cry in dismay
I hear a shot, I am gone forever more.

Kayleigh McCaffery (13)
Hartshill School

A BRIGHT SUMMER'S DAY

It was a bright summer's day
In the middle of July.
Everyone in the town had gathered
For the summer carnival.
I was looking for my friends
I saw them waiting for me on a bench.
I was on my way over to them
When the bomb went off.
It knocked me down like a bulldozer.
I got up and limped over to the bench
When I got there they were gone, gone
Forever.

Andrew West (13)
Hartshill School

HELP US!

We lie dying, dying in our sleep,
The bombs sound like thunder
coming closer, nearer.
Just as I think it's over,
I remember the only light,
I fight for life and pray for mercy.
The gunfire blazed on like
stones shattering glass,
the sound rocks my ears,
the screams flood my mind.
The blood flows thick, thicker than ink,
thicker than paint.
As dark, gloomy pictures fill my mind
I wonder can anyone help?

Duane Beers (13)
Hartshill School

MY LITTLE CHILD

Walking down the busy road, my little child and me.
Then there was a stampede as we were told there was a bomb,
We all rushed for safety to the other side of town,
We had never run so fast:
But we were running into danger.
The further we ran the more relieved we were,
We stopped as we thought we were all now safe,
Then *bang! An explosion!* So powerful the blow.
Everything went silent as we were all in shock,
I opened my eyes and turned my head to see
my little child dead.

Michelle Whitmore (13)
Hartshill School

I'M GOING

Lying there,
All I can hear are bombs
Bombs exploding on the floor
It was like the world would end
People screaming, shouting, scattering around
Where was I to go?
No family, no friends, everyone gone.
My house in ruins
All that was left was my door in flames
A bomb came down
I thought 'Am I going to die?'
I couldn't feel my arms or my legs
My own fresh blood splattered on the floor.

Leanne Reed (14)
Hartshill School

BANG! BANG!

Everyone is dying,
Blood and guts are flying,
The butcher's was bombed today.

Everyone is crying,
Relatives are dying,
The bomb went, boom, bang, bang!
Ha! Ha! Ha! Ha!
I am the IRA,
I can kick your ass today,
I will blow you up with a bomb,
Bang! Bang! Bang! Bang! Boom!

Adam Cramp (13)
Hartshill School

Death

Clouds of smoke
As grenades are thrown
It is deserted
There is no one there
Glass on the floor as windows are shattered
But yet I lie lifeless, lost, listening
Listening for sounds, any signs
But yet I lie, a civilian, a Protestant
So cold with blood around me
I can't feel my legs
My right arm is dead
All I see are shadows around me
From the flickering lights
I shout to get someone's attention
But still I get no replies
I now lie waiting for death
Today is the only day I have been scared
So scared but yet don't show it
What will happen?
Will I die?
I don't know yet, don't care
Today death came across me.

Lesley Mara (13)
Hartshill School

Autumn

Crispy brown leaves whirling to the ground,
twisting, turning down and round.
As the westerly whirlwinds blow
and while rain comes down, the rivers flow.

Animals diving for cover,
Snuggling down for another winter.
The nights draw in
and become very dark.

All I can say is, stay in until next spring.

Líesl Hill (12)
Hartshill School

WHY AM I BULLIED?

I am a normal human being,
Aren't I?
I am a good learner,
I know I am.
I am a nice person and I don't like violence,
Of course I am.
So why am I bullied?

I'm not accident prone,
Am I?
I'm not that much of a brain,
I know I'm not.
I'm not always fighting or shouting or cursing,
Of course I'm not.
So why am I bullied?

I don't go around picking on people,
Do I?
I am a good helper,
I know I am.
I don't watch horror movies and I'm not fat, just pretty,
Of course I can't and there's nothing wrong with me.
So why am I bullied?

Lisa-Marie Cope (12)
Hartshill School

THE BOMB

The sound of the blast rings in my ears,
The sweet smell of blood and people dying lingers
in the air as people scream and shout.
I hope I've killed thousands of those innocent people,
I hope they all suffer as much as possible until they die,
I hate those people,
They all think they're safe,
But they're not.
This should teach them all a lesson,
Teach them not to be so selfish,
Teach them not to be so smart,
We will kill everybody and win this war.

Simon Canning (13)
Hartshill School

IRA BRAINS

IRA brains are all the same,
no one knows better, they are always right,
Bombing, blood and death are what keep
them going, it drives them to destruction.
Bang! Bang! Guns are blazing like a
never-ending knock at the door.
What is it that drives these people?
They must be the Devil.
These people are pure evil.
Why does God not forsake these people.
If they kill, they are pure, pure evil,
or just very, very confused.

Shaun Galletly (13)
Hartshill School

A POEM ABOUT STUFF BLOWING UP AND PEOPLE DYING

The blast of the bomb rung in my ears
The sound was deafening
It felt like the world was collapsing around me
Bodies were piled up by the thousands below my feet
The only sound left was the 'drip, drip' coming from
my lifeless neighbour's house across the road
I, battered and bruised, lay dying in a pile of rubble
My once large family destroyed in seconds
Another death-bringer echoed down the streets
While sending a message to the survivors
'We'll be back.'

Chris Ballard (13)
Hartshill School

LIFELESS ON THE FLOOR

Lying there lonely on the rubble,
I saw my mum, lifeless on the floor,
I knew she was dead, I'd never feel her again,
The touch of a feather on my skin,
It was like I was empty, had nothing more to live for.
The bombs carried on falling out of the dragon sky,
But I didn't move, why should I?
They'd wrecked my life and all I saw was
My mum lying there, lifeless on the floor.

Victoria Hatcher (14)
Hartshill School

A Poem About Me - Joel Burke

Every day I get up.
I get up
To go to school,
I go to school
To learn about stuff.
Then it comes to the weekend
And I do my homework,
After my homework
I play out.
I play out with
my friend,
Then I come in
For my dinner.
And I watch
Cartoon Network for
An hour or two.
After that I watch
A movie then
Go to bed
And I do the same
the next week.

Joel Burke (11)
Hartshill School

There Was A Fly Who Was Buzzing By!

There was a fly who was buzzing by,
Which stopped for a break on a cup of tea.
My dad turned round and said with a sigh
'What is that fly doing on my tea?'
The fly looked up with his sad little eyes
As if to say 'Let me be'
But my dad did not care but said
'Bye bye' to the fly that was on his tea.

So that was the end of the buzzing fly,
When my dad did cry 'Bye bye.'
Just because he was on Dad's tea
And Dad just wouldn't let him be.

Leanne Hodgson (12)
Hartshill School

BRAVE EVAN

The children stood together, shivering,
Wrapped in thin anoraks and woolly balaclavas
They were cursing the thick mist
Which lay suspended over the town like a blanket.

Evan was lost - how were they to find him in this?
They could only see the outline of the
person who stood a metre away.
How were they to see Evan?

Little Deirdre was sobbing,
Crying for a brother who lived like a
hero in her heart.
Brave Evan, sad Evan,
Evan who sought to save them from
the Unionists.

He was lost among the dewdrops and
the mist.
Evan McCaffery was fading,
Fading like their hopes and their courage.
All they could do now was wait.

Kate Marshall (13)
Hartshill School

I Hate My Sister

One day while in the Co-op,
I saw a toy and had to stop.
A funky little pedal machine,
That I thought would be really keen.
I stepped upon the pedal stand,
I started to move,
It was so grand!
But just one slip of my foot,
And I fell straight on my butt.
Everyone started to stare,
My sister laughed, she didn't care.
'Oh my God!' I thought
I'm glad that's not the toy I bought.

Nicola Brown (11)
Hartshill School

The Day It Rained

Cold as ice
Rain as sharp as glass
Thunder as loud as a drum
Clouds as black as a hole
Lightning as bright as the sun
Wind as strong as the sea
Frightening like a bear
Noisy like a bang
Floods as deep as a river
Snow, a flock of woolly sheep.

Rachael Pickard (12)
Hartshill School

ME!

From Daddy's little girl
to pretty as a pearl.

When I was young I was taught to share
but now I'm eleven - I'm a nightmare.

Really I'm sweet as a pea
but now my parents say 'Do the tea!'

I have started at a new school
when I'm older, I want an outdoor pool.

I like to go fishing
But I have done no kissing.

Yeh! That's me!

Kristi Jane Rogers (11)
Hartshill School

OUTSIDERS

Outsiders, people who don't fit in
Outsiders, different people who don't join in
Outsiders, can be ugly, pretty, fat or thin
Outsiders, they don't have many friends
Outsiders, are normally very lonely
Outsiders, need to be welcomed in
Outsiders, can be nice, horrible, quiet or loud
Outsiders, people who nobody really knows
Outsiders, are quiet, different, lonely people.

Simon Hayllar (13)
Hartshill School

EMBARRASSING MOMENT

I was playing hide-and-seek,
Hiding from my mum,
Something came towards me.
I wondered what it was,
It came closer and . . . plop!
It hit me on the head.

I didn't faint or anything like that,
But I did kinda get a very big lump
                            on my head.

Everybody laughed at me,
And called me 'big head'
But what they didn't know was,
I had fractured my skull.

I still have to be careful,
You know, about my head.

We know it is a lot better
And I can hit a ball with it.

And nobody laughs at me.

Rebecca Bennett (11)
Hartshill School

ANIMALS

I would like lots of cats,
They would sit on the chair,
And sleep on the mats
And have long hair.

He would like some dogs,
They would like to play,
They would dance in clogs,
All night and all day.

She would like a snake,
It'd live in a tank,
And have its own lake,
And savings in a bank.

We would like a bear,
To roam the house,
Eat sitting on a chair,
We'd call him Klaus.

Hayley Wilson (12)
Hartshill School

DR LOVE

From the day he popped out of his mum,
He's always been different to some
See he's as mad as a hatter for women,
And is always crazy for a lady,
One thing for sure, he'll always score -
He goes out pulling daily!

He's cool as a cucumber,
Smooth, y'know - on the ball!
Certainly smitten and obsessed -
And doesn't get turned down at all!
Babyface-like - emm - a baby
Charming like a prince.
He kissed a woman once . . .
And hasn't failed since.

And never ever will!

Adam Nicholls (12)
Hartshill School

My Embarrassing Moment

I was three and a half,
And I was having a laugh,
We were going to Paignton,
On a minibus.

I was with my mum, auntie, brother and dad,
Stepbrother, stepsister and grandad.
We got there (finally) after our five-hour trip,
Then we went to the sea and had a dip.
We were doing the things a normal family would,
I was being mischievous as much as I could.

I went running round the fish pond like I'd been told not to,
Suddenly I was all wet and I'd lost my shoe.

Richard Moore (11)
Hartshill School

My Embarrassing Moment

I was nine and a half
I was having a laugh,
playing cricket, playing cricket.
When all of a sudden
down came my trousers
playing cricket, playing cricket.
Then I threw the ball at
the wicket, playing cricket.

Adam Hartshorn (11)
Hartshill School

O' Mighty Rainforest

                 The
               Mighty
            Rainforest
       Rules the kingdom.
      Its green atmosphere
     Holds wildlife that live on
    To a long race of creatures.
   The cascading waterfalls fill
  Me with ecstasy and pleasant joy.
 Its enchanting rivers are beautiful,
Silent magic, and somehow so like a weird
Fantasy that lives on for many a decade.
Green captures the rain forest more than the rest of the
Plants that use browns and magic colours to impress the rulers.

Mark Roach (11)
Hartshill School

Stress Attack

I'm 'Stressed Harry', that's me
My eyes are blurred as you may see
Don't get in the way
I could knock you down
And you might end up looking like a clown
I can't control myself, I need some help
I trod on my own toe the other day
And gave out a 'yelp'!
My hair has grown back
Since I pulled it out
My normal life has just gone
              down the spout!

Terri Pratt (12)
Hartshill School

HALLOWE'EN

The 31st of October
We all cry out
The ghouls and ghosts
Fly all about

This is the time
For spooks
And all things horrid
And things like that

In the evening
Children play trick or treat
They collect lots of money
And plenty of sweets

Dressed up in their costumes
They knock on your door
Trying to scare you
To get lots more

The witches cast magic
And make lots of spells
While children are sleeping
Tight and well.

Sammi Smith (12)
Hartshill School

MY POEM
A POSH JOSH WITH DOSH

There was a boy called Josh
everyone thought he was rather posh
even though he had no dosh.

But how could Josh
be very posh
if he never had any dosh?

Josh's brain said to Josh
'Everyone thinks I'm rather posh,
so I should be able to get some dosh
if I act very posh.'

Josh was walking back from school,
walking very posh,
then suddenly he spotted some dosh,
then he thought *I'm called Josh,*
I have got a bit of dosh
and I am very posh . . .

Josh suddenly shouted out
'I'm a posh Josh with dosh!'

Louisa Mitchell (12)
Hartshill School

My Fear!

My mum has booked a holiday
I hope it's not abroad.
You see, I'm terrified of planes.
Can you catch a train to Spain?

I'm sitting in the airport
People are buzzing all around.
They all seem very excited
While I think I'll be stuck to the ground.

We're standing in a queue
A queue to board the plane.
I've got my lucky charm with me
I hope it keeps me sane.

We're high, high in the sky
It isn't really that bad.
I'm even eating apple pie
And I thought I would be sad.

Laura Duggins (12)
Hartshill School

Barney

B is my little big dog
A nd jumps around like a big frog
R ound and round he'll chase his stump
N ext to Dad he'll do a trump.
E ars as big, they look like a wig
Y es, he is Barney and he is my doggie
      Did I mention that he is a Rottie?

Wesley Green (12)
Hartshill School

SOUTH PARK

S outh Park is a little town
O n the edge of the
U niverse.
T ill you visit you will not know it's on a
H ill.

P rincipal Victoria is very mean
A s good as can be. It's
R eally good when Kenny gets
K illed.

James Stewart (12)
Hartshill School

TO PLAY WITH A DOG

First of all you need a ball and lead.
And then a dog to play with these.
Then go to a park, on a sunny day.
It must be a sunny day.
Then you let the dog be free, by letting it off its lead.
And then, only then, toss the ball in the air.
They will jump very high and take it from the sky.
If they bark they're having fun.
But if they don't . . . stop playing.
After a while, put them back on the lead and go back home.
When you get home, let them have a drink, then give them a treat.
Yes a treat! For being so good.
Then put the lead and ball away - until another day.

Gemma Burke (13)
Kenilworth School

DEAD OF NIGHT

I woke in the dead of night
Feeling heavy, yet feeling light.
I got out of my safe warm bed
And suddenly saw something burning red.
It crept across the creaking floor,
And snuck out of my open door.
I charged out after it, starting to cry.
Who was it? What? Where and why?

I charged downstairs, running fast,
Catching a glimpse of his purple cast,
It raced into the living room,
Showing me its face of doom.
I followed him to our dining room,
Where I saw what looked like brooms.
I saw them, they had thousands of eyes,
Who were they? What? Where and why?

They all had eyes, millions - blue.
Bigger than ours. Oh what shall I do?
They started to talk in a language unknown,
They shot up in what looked like cones.
What happened to them? Where did they go?
What should I do, I do not know!
Who shall I tell? Should it be Vi?
Who where they? What? Where and why?

Alison Gregory (11)
Kenilworth School

I Have A Dream

I have a dream . . .
That the lady in green is an Eco warrior,
Climbing every mountain,
Swimming every sea.

She lives in the trees
Gazing at the sun,
Believing nature's beauty.
Until day is done.

The rind of green undergrowth
Hides her warrior's skin
She sees the prowling tigers
She loves the sharks that swim.

She dives into the raging sea
Devoured by its waves
Swimming with dolphins every day
Then, lying in the caves.

Returning to her tree house
She sees her best friend - Bird
She feeds him very silently
So her love for him is heard.

Her beauty's nothing to her
There's more than that in life
She'd rather be killed than the animals,
When the poacher lifts his knife.

Clare Haley (12)
Kenilworth School

What's Wrong With Me?

I'm blue, I'm black
My heads at the back

I'm purple and green
And I'm not clean

Oh no, oh no, oh what shall I do?
I know what I'll do,I'll watch channel two

Oh yes, oh yes, I've gotta do that
I'll watch it tonight while I eat cow pat

That's fair you see
You won't notice me

I'll stay there forever
And we'll die together.

Luke Hollingsworth (11)
Kenilworth School

Rosie

Her hair is blonde,
Her eyes dull brown.
Her temper rides faster than a raging wolf;
Her anger sinks deeper than a biting thorn.

Once roused she is slow to cool,
If you think she forgets, then thou art a fool.
And yet the time to fear her is when she dons a sweet face,
Then you know she's planning something,
Possibly involving Mace.

To err is human, as is to forgive and forget.
Now, she will do none of these things as yet.
Till, perhaps, she requires this of another,
Then methinks she will begin to learn
That not all other life is to kick and spurn.
But mayhap . . . I will learn!

William Mack (13)
Kenilworth School

IZZY FROM WOILS

When I land down on your planet
Please don't get the spooks
I'm a very friendly alien
I've just got funny looks.

I know I've got spots all over me
And no, they are not boils
They are not contagious
They are quite fashionable in Woils.

Upon my antennae
Are perched my big brown eyes
I know they look quite scary
But they're good for spotting flies.

I have like you two arms and legs
Two feet and two hands
In fact I'm quite like the people
Who live on your lands.

So when I come to meet you
Please shake hands and say hello
I'm a very friendly alien
Who's a green and yellow little fellow!

Melanie Taylor (11)
Kenilworth School

THE FUNERAL
(In memory of my grandma)

The organ started . . .
We walked in and sat down on the front pew.
The stale, musty smell of the church was sickening.
I swallowed and looked down at my programme.
Knowing then, I didn't want to be there,
I stood up with the rest of the congregation
to sing the first hymn.
As I opened my mouth, I could feel the tears
starting to sting my eyes.
Before I knew it
I was crying
I was crying
The feeling of loneliness washed over me.
The despair fought against my soul.
I was crying and I couldn't stop.

The last dredges of her life are sealed in a little box
somewhere underground.
One half of my life has shut its door
and passed away from me.
I couldn't have stopped it; she's gone forever.
The pain is a never-ending heartache.
The loneliness is a never-ending fight with my happiness.
I'm alone . . . I'm frightened,
And there's nothing to stop this feeling.

Clare Webster (13)
Kenilworth School

I HAVE A DREAM

I would like to paint the sky light pink
The buzz of bees on the march, the sound of
Seagulls in thin air.
Hear the music of shooting stars zooming through midnight
I have a dream to capture the past and keep it in a
Moses jar.
If I could, I would paint a snowflake black as tar
I have a dream to taste gravity on the end of a
Giant's fork.
The heat of a candle in the middle of the night, I would like
To hear the sunset going below the hills.
I wish I could listen to the paint dry under the floor
Boards of a big black thunder cloud.
I have a dream to taste sunset maybe after noon
I wish I had a bank full of willow trees I wish I could
Stop time. *I had a dream*, to open up the heavens I
Have a dream, I have a dream.

Ben Spann (14)
North Leamington School

I HAVE A DREAM

I have a dream
About ice-cream
A flavour of the moon.
If only you could hold the sun
If only you could jump and run over the horizon,
I have a dream of tasting magic
To feel its glow and sparkle
I have a dream of moving time
I have a dream of a talking line.

Gavin Ranson (12)
North Leamington School

My Dream, My Wish

I have a dream . . .
I want to touch time gone by,
I want to smell the beams of sun,
I want to touch the stars in the night sky
And capture them forever.

I have a wish . . .
I want to see a breath of wind,
I want to taste the sunset on a warm
Summer's day,
I want to see the music move from
The radio to my ear.

I have a dream . . .
I want to walk on the fluffy clouds,
I want to capture summer of 1999
In a big glass jar
I want to touch colours of spring.
I have a dream, I have a wish.

Emma Mortimer (13)
North Leamington School

The Accuracy Of A Hawk

I have a dream . . .
That I could run as fast as the world rotates,
That I could hear the thoughts of my mates,
That I could taste the golden reflection on the lake,
That I could see through the eyes of a slithering snake,
That I could eat the moon off my fork,
That I could capture accuracy of a hawk,
I have a dream . . .

Quentin Oury (12)
North Leamington School

I Have A Dream

I have a dream
to taste the dew
on the early morning grass,
I have a dream to smell the moon
and to see the corn grow,
I have a dream to touch the sky
and see time go by,
I have a dream to smell the sun
and to smell the darkness go on and on.
I have a dream to taste the clouds
and to touch the moon,
I have a dream to taste Saturn
and see the world go round and round.

Sophie Huckvale (12)
North Leamington School

My Dream

I have a dream to touch the sky and eat
the clouds of candyfloss, to capture the sun
in a cookie jar.
I have a dream, to lick off all the sugary
twinkles of the stars.
To surf on the Milky Way of the galaxy
I have a dream to fly around,
to glide around
to jump from plant to plant,
to find new worlds,
I have a dream to paint the rainbow.

Sybella Davis (12)
North Leamington School

I Have A Dream

I have a dream,
That I can hold the sunset,
In a glass jar and watch the world
Go by in my jar,
I wish I could taste the orange of the sun.
I wish I could ride on the back of a
Bee as it flies on its journey of life.
I wish I could blow out each candle
In the sky.
I wish I could taste the fire at the
Golden sun.
I wish I could hide the night moon
Under my pillow and keep the sun in
My jar under my bed.
I'd like to taste the fear at the
Screaming monkey and see from the eyes
Of the cobra snake.

I have a dream!

Chris Halfpenny (14)
North Leamington School

I Have A Dream

I have a dream of a dreamy lad from France
Who's always kept in a trance
He sits there all day
With nothing to say
He could be dreaming of me
What's the chance?

Sam Hargraves (13)
North Leamington School

I HAVE A DREAM

I had a dream I'd go to the moon
What do I see?
What do I smell?
What do I hear?
What can I touch?
I see white, white, white,
Everywhere is white.
I smell something strange
Like I've never smelt before
I hear nothing.
Everywhere is still, still, still,
I touch the moon
I feel soft powdery moon.
I feel lonely, lonely, lonely,
Can I go home now, *yes!*
I had a dream.

Emma Metcalfe (12)
North Leamington School

I HAD A DREAM

I had a dream.
I had a dream to touch the sun,
We could hear the clouds float on,
I'd like to hear the sound of the wind,
To feel the rays of the moon.
To see the world compact and small,
To taste time whiz on.
To feel everyone's emotions,
I had a dream that my dream came true.

Jonny Ayres (12)
North Leamington School

I Have A Dream

As the light goes out
And I snuggle into bed
I drift into a deep sleep,
I wish I could wake the moon
And extinguish the last of the sun.

In my mind I push the stars
Out past the darkness towards
The sky beyond
As the glow of the last star
Drifts away to the sky beyond.

Darkness sets on the earth below
Then suddenly there was a roar
And a flash of light.
I got out of bed and walked
Over to the window, pulled back
The curtains.
There was the moon and the stars and the sun
A gust coming into sight,
Over the dew fields
I have a dream.

Nathan Batchelor (14)
North Leamington School

Dreaming

I have a dream,
I smelt the wind, it was fresh,
I saw the colour of the music,
I tasted the sweet taste of happiness,
I felt the clouds, soft and light,
I heard the joy of the trees.

But instead,
All I smell is the disgusting scent of hate,
All I see is the pollution,
All I taste is the bitterness of pain,
All I feel are the words of anger,
All I hear is the earth crying.

Samuel Hayler (14)
North Leamington School

DREAM ON

I have a dream to swim the
oceans with a school of dolphins and
capture their call in a shell and hang
it round my neck. I touched a rainbow
and tasted its colours, I collected the pot
of gold when I reached the end. From
out of the darkness I reached the stars
and smelt their glowing light, it was
so bright, I licked the surface, it tasted
nice like sugar and spice. I picked up
the Millennium Dome and took it home
to put out on display. I spoke to the
flowers and they sang back to me and I
waved to the buzzing bee. I caught
the sunshine in the palm of my hand,
it was so soft like melted sand.
I picked up hate and threw it away,
then invited love to come and stay!
I have a dream that this dream will
last forever.

Amy Tucker (13)
North Leamington School

I HAVE A DREAM

I have a dream,
Of hearing a butterfly gently land on a petal,
Of walking on a cloud and touching the blue sky,
Of waking up and seeing the sun glistening through
The window.
To taste the fire as it flickers in the moonlight.

I have a dream,
Of stealing the darkness from the night and keeping it in
A glass jar.
Of capturing the last breath of a ladybird as it expires
In the early morning dew.
Of becoming the autumn breeze and whistling through
The trees,
To raise the spirits of the dead and setting them
Free forever.

I have a dream.

Rachael Chesworth (12)
North Leamington School

CANDYFLOSS CLOUDS

I have a dream to eat the doughnut ring around Uranus.
I want to find the ten pence moon in the couch.
I wish I could feel the buzz of lively music.
I would like to hear the soothing rays of light in an early sunrise.
I want to taste the pink candyfloss clouds of sunset.
I wish I could swim through the ocean treetops of the Amazon
                                                    rainforest.
I have a dream to heal all suffering with the huge sheet of the night sky.

James White (13)
North Leamington School

TO TASTE GOD'S LAUGHTER

I have a dream
Here on the earth
To watch the sun rotating
To taste the smell of fire
To smell my own desire.

I have a dream
To walk on water
To watch me float
To smell salt water
To taste God's laughter.

I have a dream
To walk on the air
To smell exhaust fumes
To watch the TV in the air
To taste candyfloss in the sun.

Tracey Talbot (12)
North Leamington School

I HAVE A DREAM

I want to taste the rainbow, I want to feel the sun,
I want to smell the magic from a witch,
I want to hear the snow whistle along.
I want to feel the moon, I want to taste the future,
I want to hear the paint go plop, plop,
I want to smell the rocks crackle and pop.
I want to hear the darkness,
I want to smell the time
I have a dream!
I have a dream!

Jamie Williams (12)
North Leamington School

I Have A Dream

I have a dream
I'm flying in the air, it feels
Sensational, there's birds all around
Me, it's just incredible.
The clouds look so fluffy, they're
Just like candyfloss, I wouldn't
Want to eat them though, in case
They fall and drop.
I'm looking down beneath me, I
Don't see a thing, it's just clouds,
Clouds, and more clouds, thank God.
I can't hear my sister sing.
I'm flying really fast now, the
Wind's rushing in my face, my
Eyes are filling with water and
My mouth is just like paste.
The birds are still beside me,
They look really cute, their feathers
Are nice and neat, it looks like a
Posh suit. I looked straight above
And heard some bells ring, I see
Some glittering angels and one of
Them looking at me.
My dream is over now and I've just
Woken up, life just feels so
Boring, but who cares, that's life
And it's tough.
I have a dream.

Sabrina Savariar (12)
North Leamington School

My Dream

I had a dream of flying to the moon
And smelling heaven.
I wish I could see the future of my life.
I wish I could touch the Olympic flame,
Burning high in the sky.
I had one big dream,
To feel what it's like to be a professional footballer,
But still I have many other dreams.
The most special one of all,
Feeling the passion in 1960-1970,
When Manchester United won the European Cup
And best of all when England won the World Cup.

Andrew Ward (13)
North Leamington School

I Have A Dream

I have a dream,
To smell, taste and hear things,
That once were only seen.

To taste the sound of the birds in the rainforest,
And the gush of a river down the rocky mountainside.
The whistle of the wind through the waving trees,
And the dropping of the leaves when they have died.

To touch the smell of the roast dinner in the kitchen,
And the scent of the rose just bloomed.
The smell of fresh bread wafting through the door,
And the sound of peace after war.

I have a dream.

Jackie Perry (12)
North Leamington School

I Have A Dream

I have a dream,
that I could paint the world,
multicoloured.
I could see through walls
and taste the sun.
I wish I could hear the shooting stars,
as they shot across the sky,
and feel the moon.
What do the clouds taste like?
Fluffy and sweet like candyfloss.
And how does the sun shine?
I wish I could fly through the sky like a bird with silver wings,
and taste the harsh bark of a tree.
I have a dream I could touch the sky and taste lightning.
I want to capture the wind and put it in my pocket,
so when it is hot, I can take it out and there will be
a fresh breeze.
I want to snatch the clouds out of the sky,
and paint them bright blue.
I have a dream.

Harriet Whitehead (12)
North Leamington School

I Have A Dream

I want to touch a sunbeam
I want to taste the moon,
Taste the air in my room.

I want to touch the stars,
Or even taste Mars.

I want to feel the darkness,
Or even taste goodness.

I want to feel the sun,
To taste the sun.

I want to see moonlight,
To feel light.

I have a dream.

Laura Wilkins (13)
North Leamington School

NEW MOON

I have a dream to smash the moonlight,
And watch it fall from the sky.
I want to take a piece home and listen to it in the night,
I should like to kick the wind,
To see it bowl across the land.
Sweep up the moments into a ball,
And blow them away across the earth.
I want a bank of memories,
To open each box and reminisce.
I want to replay the moment, the taste, the sound.
I want to paint a picture of the sound of a brand new day,
I want to feel the dawns of days that have passed
I want to switch off time,
Touch the stillness,
Taste the darkness,
And smell the sensation.
I should like to taste the passage of time.
I want to fly through 2000 ages,
I want to see the future.

Mary Addyman (13)
North Leamington School

I Dream To Dream Until I Die

I dream to dream until I die,
I wish to touch the starry sky.
I have a dream to see Mother Nature,
She could teach me to paint time,
So I could smell the past and touch the future.
I want to see the song of a whale
And trap it in a glass bottle.
Then throw it out to sea.
I want to smell the excitement of the millennium,
And touch to Jupiter's red eye.
I wish to sleep in a hammock woven by a spider,
I want to smell the rattlesnake's poison.
I wish to know the meaning of life.
I dream to dream until I die
I wish to touch the starry sky,
I want to taste the seasons and the weather,
I dream to dream forever and ever.

Alice Griffin (13)
North Leamington School

I Have A Dream

I have a dream,
To taste the smell of drying paint,
To hear the sound of people thinking,
To smell the sound of the wind,
I want to touch the smell of roses,
Touch gravity and hear the stars,
Or taste the sun,
Maybe even see the smell of Swiss cheese.

Ian Garrett (13)
North Leamington School

AN IMAGINATIVE JOURNEY THROUGH TIME

I have a dream to see the journey of a flower
From germination to wilting
The sound of the crisp petals falling off.
I wish I could taste the sweet pollen
Just dripping on to the tip of my tongue.

If only I could reach out and grab a planet
A planet with tastes, sounds and smells,
A planet like Mars
With caramel and chocolate for afters.

If only I could taste the Milky Way of stars,
Spending each day cutting a star in half.
Tasting the wonderful sounds it made.
Licking the crunchy topping off the top.

If only I could taste the sounds of a whale singing.
The sweet noises should taste like sherbet,
(As it's sweet as sweet can be)
Enjoying each second of it slowly.

If only I could catch the darkness,
The cloudy, powdery, black substance.
In a bottle and keep it under my pillow,
And open it each time I wanted a good dream.

If only . . .

Nisha Rai (13)
North Leamington School

I Have A Dream

To catch a fly while it's buzzing around
in its own world.
To see what the words heaven and hell mean.
To taste the raindrops as they slowly enter the atmosphere.
To hear a candle burn while the wax is
melting and dripping to the ground.
To touch the sky when I reach my long
enormous arms into the cold air.
To smell the sun while it's burning
away in the galaxy.
To take a tiny bite out of the stars
just shining there quiet and silent.
To catch a bird and secure it away
in my treasure chest in the corner
of my bedroom.
To taste the planet Saturn's rings just
as quiet as can be.
To touch the sunset while it goes
Down into the other part of the world.
To see the air just floating around
in the environment.
To paint the wind as it approaches my
soft cold face.

Kathryn Riley (12)
North Leamington School

I Have A Dream

I have a dream
I dream I can hear the future,
And keep the sound in my mind.
I dream I can taste lightning,
And keep the taste in a box.
I dream I can touch the sky,
And keep the feeling in my mind.
I dream I can stop time,
And start again whenever I want.
I dream I can sit on clouds,
And stay up there forever.
Sadly I only dream these things,
They will never happen,
But maybe they will,
In my mind.

Katie Travis (12)
North Leamington School

I Have A Dream

I have a dream
That I can paint the sound of a burning candle,
To taste the sunset,
Or to smell the darkness,
To smell the success of happiness,
Or to touch a star,
To reach out and touch the fresh spring air,
Or to eat the smell of roses,
To ride on the rings of Saturn,
Or to fly like a bird on the wind.

This is my dream!

Richard Evans (13)
North Leamington School

MEMORIES IN THE STARS

I have a dream of future days
Of keeping the past in my pocket
Of capturing the last breath of the dragonfly
Of saving my memories in the night's stars
To remember when I look to the sky.

I have a dream of living forever and missing nothing
Of feeling the happiness of the laughing child
Of walking through paintings into that world
Of saving my feelings in a biscuit tin
To remember with every bite.

I have a dream of living the books I read
Of being the every day breeze
Of tasting the crispness of autumn leaves
Of saving my thoughts on the legs of a centipede
To remember when it scuttles past.

I have a dream of nightmares being banned
Of wars being killed
Of the world being as perfect as the butterfly on a petal
Of happiness being stored in the bank
To spend whenever it's needed.

Miranda Forth (12)
North Leamington School

My Extraordinary Millennium Dream

I have a dream to be extraordinary,
To taste the Seven Wonders of the World.

To smell the pyramids,
Or munch a sample of Ephesus.

To catch the four elements in a glass jam jar,
Or taste fire and smell the earth from afar.

Maybe I could lock all these adventures in
A time capsule,
Then relive them in the new millennium.

I want to touch the sky, taste the clouds and
Hear the stars,
This is my extraordinary, millennium dream.

Kohinoor Meghji (12)
North Leamington School

Skate Mate

Skating around is really cool.
Go to a skate park and drop a vert or to a foam pit
Where you don't get hurt.
Do flips and tricks and skate about.
Pick up speeds and turn and shout.
Mind you don't slip or fall over.
It's fun when you drop a ramp you can feel your
Wheels hovering about.
And on the other side you can do a trick and your
Radical friends have a fit.

Alistair McLeod (12)
St Benedict's RC High School, Alcester

The Smugglers

A man with a lantern
Flashes a light,
To warn those on shore
We're coming tonight.

They watch and they wait
Not saying a word
Until the sound
Of the oars are heard.

Then quickly they hurry
Into the cave
To smuggle the diamonds
How brave, how brave.

Big drums of rum
Were hidden in the cave,
Right at the back they
Worked like slaves.

Away they went not saying a word,
The sea and the wind
Could only be heard.

Hazel Truscott (11)
St Benedict's RC High School, Alcester

Lesson Time

Little children in a classroom
Children working, children not
Children looking at the clock
Waiting till they're told to stop.

Busy writing with their pens,
Adding hundreds, units, tens,
Glancing at the corner clock
Working till they're told to stop.

Stephen Capron (12)
St Benedict's RC High School, Alcester

FUTURE VOICES - FUN IN THE SUN

We're on the beach in summer
Enjoying our holiday
The sun is blazing hot
Ice-creams are on the way!

We're relaxing round the pool
With a cool drink in our hand
As I take a sip from my glass
I listen to the band!

I get up to play beach ball
As I've topped up on my tan
I jump and take a shot
And it lands with a bang!

I go back to relaxing
Round the pool
The sun is blazing hot
So I use my fan to keep me cool!

I close my eyes
And think of all the
Fun in the sun.

Charlotte Richards (13)
St Benedict's RC High School, Alcester

The Match

I love Manchester United
As I walk down the ever so familiar Sir Matt Busby Way,
The streets bursting with ecstatic United fans and
Burly police officers on huge armoured horses.
Today's opponents are Wimbledon,
And I've just got the match programme.
Around the stadium you can hear Manchester
United radio blaring through your ears.
I get into my seat, pushing my way through the gangway.
I hear a great roar as Ferguson's Red Army
Appear from the tunnel.
2-0 the final score,
Yorke and Cole, the scorers in a great match.
On the way home I brought a poster before
Catching the Metrolink back to Sale.

Michael Gurrie (12)
St Benedict's RC High School, Alcester

Creativity

Oh dear God you helped me make,
A very special birthday cake.
I weighed the flour, eggs and sugar,
To bake this cake for my mother.

Another day I took a sheet
And folded it very neat.
I formed a brilliant aeroplane
For me to play with again and again.

I went to college for the day
They gave me some soil and a tray.
In the soil, I planted some seeds
The garden I made had no weeds.

Thank you God for my hands,
So I can create all my plans,
And all the talents you gave me,
So I can have such creativity.

Joel Brimmell (11)
St Benedict's RC High School, Alcester

AUTUMN

The wind is blowing,
Autumn is showing,
The leaves are falling,
Onto the grass.
The summer has gone,
The trees start to die,
The birds are cold,
So away they fly!
To warmer places they will go,
Where all the trees,
Have leaves to show,
Where the sun is out,
With people about,
But as for here,
People disappear.

Jenny Miller (12)
St Benedict's RC High School, Alcester

THE CALVARY CRISIS

He carried the cross to Calvary,
However, should He fall,
He'd be beaten and whipped and mocked and kicked,
He was Jesus, Lord of all.

He accepted a painful death on the cross,
He was sent to be crucified.
Although God knew it was Man's loss,
Our Lord and Saviour died.

Then Joseph of Arimathea came,
He came with a request.
He asked for Jesus' body so he
Could put Our Lord to rest.

On Easter Sunday the prophets were right,
Our Lord was truly blest!
For afterwards He came into sight
Of those who loved Him best!

And even now, we celebrate
The day Our Lord has risen,
We remember today in our own special ways
The things that He has given.

Jimmy Marino (11)
St Benedict's RC High School, Alcester

THE MARATHON

Gun goes off,
I start off slow,
But further on,
I start to go.

I'm going faster,
I start to speed,
I'm passing runners,
I'm in the lead!

It's getting tough now,
Someone's catching me,
He's running faster,
It's easy to see.

I'm second place now,
I'm slowing a lot,
I can't go for much longer,
And it's really hot.

At last it's finished,
I'm really tired now,
I lost first place,
I can't see how.

David Whittaker (12)
St Benedict's RC High School, Alcester

MY TOYS

A rattle, a teddy, my teething ring
A thing on the door where I can swing
Building bricks soon took their place
Then little cars for me to race.

Lego came when I was three
And jigsaw puzzles just for me
An Action Man with guns and swords
Another Barbie - my sister hoards.

Things start changing when I reach ten
Super Nes now not Action Men
A PlayStation and a hand-held game
My life can never be the same.

Callum McCormick (12)
St Benedict's RC High School, Alcester

MY POEM

If you listen, what can you hear?
I can hear talking, laughter, giggling and shouting.
Everyone seems to be yelling,
The noise is deafening.
I can't hear myself think.
Everything's moving,
It's going so fast,
The cars are zooming past my window,
Aeroplanes are flying over my head,
It's all going on while I am trying
To sleep in my bed.
Is the world stopping, is it slowing down?
No it just carries on going around and around.

Helen Boffey (12)
St Benedict's RC High School, Alcester

SUPPLY TEACHER

Here is the rule for what not to do
Whenever your teacher has the flu,
Or for another reason stays in bed
(tut tut)
And a different teacher comes instead
(dun, dun, dun . . .)

When the new teacher at last arrives
Takes the register to see who's on the
Skive,
Begins the lesson with some maths
John and Bob are stifling their laughs.

Elsie and Jane are chewing the forbidden
Gum,
When really they're supposed to be working
Out a sum.

The teacher is going spare
Almost tearing out her hair,
She screams, 'I've had enough,'
She grabs her bags and hat
And says,
'That is that!'

Luisa Petta (11)
St Benedict's RC High School, Alcester

Future Voices

Transport, how will it change?

Cars, boats, planes,
Bicycles, buses, trains.

Will we have new transport like hovering cars?

Land speed record, will it be fast?
How long will the latest one last?

Will an aeroplane when in mid-flight
Be powered by electricity maybe, or light?

Will we be riding everywhere on bikes
Or maybe going on long hikes?

Will we be able to land on Mars?

Day trips to the moon.
When will it happen?
Hopefully, soon.

George Godding (13)
St Benedict's RC High School, Alcester

The Countryside

Blackberries glistening in the hedgerow,
In the distance I hear the cock crow.
It has been raining all the day,
The farmer's rushing to harvest the hay.

In the field the sheep are bleating,
The pheasants cackle and the cat is sleeping,
The sheep stop their grazing and stare at me,
The ducks ignore us and carry on with their tea.

The combine harvester is slowing down,
The corn is going to the town,
It goes to make our daily bread,
If it wasn't for the countryside,
We wouldn't get fed!

Katherine Millward (11)
St Benedict's RC High School, Alcester

SATURDAY

Up early, stables today.
Get to the stables have some fun,
A perfect Saturday morning.
Have a riding lesson,
Learn a lot.
Mum's here, time to go home.

Back at home,
Have some lunch and a quick rest.
Do my homework, maths and FT.
Boring, boring, boring.
Finished at last.
Go upstairs read my magazines and listen to the radio,
This is more like it!

Dinner time!
Spaghetti Bolognese, my favourite.
Watch TV then time for bed.

Katherine Mann (12)
St Benedict's RC High School, Alcester

My Poem Of The Seasons

Summer
Summer is the best.
Cycling with my friends,
Then I have a rest.
Busy bee's making food all those hours.
Oh I love the smell of all those flowers.

Autumn
Autumn leaves changing colour,
Falling on the roads,
Squirrels gathering fallen nuts,
And then they hide loads.

Winter
Winter soon coming,
Christmas is coming.
Hot meals at the door.
Jack Frost on the floor.

Spring
Spring is here
Birds busy making nests
Flowers popping up for a rest.
First glimpse of the morning sun.
Oh how life is fun.

Lewis Williams (11)
St Benedict's RC High School, Alcester

DEPRESSION

She sits there in a corner
A corner on her own.

She stands by the wall at playtime
With no feelings to show.

She hides everything away
And locks up all her gifts.

She throws away the key
In a very shallow ditch.

When people try to talk
She runs and hides away.

It's as if she hides herself for ever
In a secret place far away.

One day when I was playing
I noticed she had gone.

'Gone where?' I wondered to myself,
Gone . . . Gone . . . Gone.

Anne Gould-Fellows (11)
St Benedict's RC High School, Alcester

GRANDFATHER'S CLOCK

In my house stands an old grandfather clock,
In the middle of the night it strikes thirteen,
I'm the only one who knows this,
I plan to keep it this way.

I creep downstairs, I feel someone watching me,
But I know it's only the eyes,
It's the eyes of the grandfather that are watching me,
He sends a spine-tingling shiver down the back of me.

I step steadily into the lounge and hide around the corner,
Then all of a sudden there is a whirring noise,
An opening in the wall appears,
It leads to the most mind-blowing place.

There are people ready to show you around,
Me, I know my way around.
To the left, a tree in the shape of a clock,
Not an ordinary tree, it never will die.

To the front is the most spectacular sight,
It's a gold fountain resembling a peacock,
The water that comes out is pure silver,
If you wish hard enough it might come true.

Every night only one hour to spare
I visit a dream world that's not really there
I go out the door and creep around the corner,
Waiting for me is the grandfather.

Mimi Fisher (12)
St Benedict's RC High School, Alcester

CAN YOU HEAR THE SOUND OF . . .?

Can you hear the sound of
Lions roaring for their food,
Snakes hissing along the path,
Hippos thumping, as they wade in the mud?

Can you hear the sound of
Waves crashing along the seashore,
Splash, splash, people swimming in the sea
Everyone rushing at the sound of an ice-cream van?

Can you hear the sound of
Rain trickling upon your roof
Wind howling as it sways the trees,
Hailstones bouncing off the ground?

Can you hear the sound of
Rustling leaves blown across the ground
Birds chirping in their nests
Owls hooting up in the trees?

Can you hear the sound of
Mums chattering as they drop off at school
Bells ringing, it's the start of school
Children laughing in the playground?

Rachael Jones (12)
St Benedict's RC High School, Alcester

Sony

Sony makes all kind of things,
Computer peripherals are my favourite ones,
Sony.
They make the Sony PlayStation,
Which I play cool games on,
Sony
Make the super woofer,
That is a speaker - there isn't one cooler,
Sony.
Super hi-fi's are their games,
So the music better not be lame.
Sony.
Super TVs are sometimes named,
After famous writers so they claim,
Super Sony.

Ian Burnip (12)
St Benedict's RC High School, Alcester

Future Voices

Footballs fly in all directions during training sessions,
Food flies at school dinner time
Vegetable fights across the floor,
Birmingham City matches, that's where tempers fly,
Kingfisher Colts will fly through the League,
Lunchtime flies when you're having fun,
Playing football in the sun,
The Man City keeper flies through the air,
Then the Ipswich striker pulls out his hair,
Magazines fly when you make them into planes.

Daniel Houston (12)
St Benedict's RC High School, Alcester

STOKE AND LIFE

Once every Saturday afternoon,
I enter another world,
A world full of mystery, excitement,
wonder, drama and passion,
A world which is Stoke City.
Entering the ground is entering heaven,
I walk up the steps and stop,
To anticipate the wondrous buzz,
Inside me is a wonderful joy,
This joy is the reason I salvage a smile,
I walk on and take my seat,
How I still wonder, think and smile,
is what I wonder every night,
Will things ever improve?
Or will I have to struggle on in this difficult time?
My scarf is wrapped round on my neck, keeping me warm,
keeping my joy.
But the key to my joy is found by depressing depression, the
very moment the opposition score.
I trek on for an hour praying for a goal which may unlock the
depression and welcome back joy.
The final whistle blows and I know I'm deprived of my joy
for another week,
What once was heaven is now hell.

Sam La Vedrine (12)
St Benedict's RC High School, Alcester

TV

I love TV it's my friend,
It drives my family round the bend.
Grand Prix racing it's amazing,
Jean Alesi he loves a little racy.
And the commentators are really crazy,
Now Homer Simpson thinks he's buff,
But he drinks too much duff.
Cartman, Stan and Kyle, they come from South Park,
And in class Mr Garrison gives them a good mark,
Now onto WWF
When they speak into the microphones they must go deaf,
And Chandler and Joey sharing a flat,
But then Pheobe came in and gave them a slap,
I love TV it's so cool
Everyone shout 'TV rules!'

John Partridge (13)
St Benedict's RC High School, Alcester

WHERE AM I?

Where am I?
I hear voices but they are not familiar
Where am I?
I see people but they don't seem to see me
Everybody in white
Where am I?
Is it a wedding? *No!*

Where am I?
Everybody looks the same
Everyone has white skin
Everybody (even boys!) Wears a white dress
Where am I?
Is it heaven? *Yes!*

Can anyone see me?
Am I invisible?
Is it all a dream?
Will I wake up soon?
I can't be in heaven yet can I?
Or can I?

Vicky Bostock (12)
St Benedict's RC High School, Alcester

NATURE

All the animals begin to call
Whether they be short or tall.
Horses leaping, showing their moves
Zebras with their flying hooves.

They all begin to come out.

Other animals begin to call
Smaller animals come out to crawl,
Baby birds love to shout
As the mother darts about.

They all begin to come out.

Smaller animals begin to call
As they take a tumble or fall,
Fish are squirming and splashing
Crocodiles jaws are always gnashing.

They all begin to come out.

Gemma Ludlow (12)
St Benedict's RC High School, Alcester

LIFE

I'm a carefree person - I suppose
Just taking life as it comes.
I'm out for that moment -
Not the past, nor the future,
Just the present.
Okay - maybe sometimes I think
What will the future hold for me?
Mmmm I wonder what will happen to me
Maybe I'll marry, maybe I won't
Maybe I'll have kids, maybe I won't.
Maybe I'll be divorced at forty
I don't know - who cares.
Live for now, not later or what's gone already,
Live your life, don't lose it.

Sophie Cooter (13)
St Benedict's RC High School, Alcester

BAD FISH

My fish is very naughty,
It eats stuff fishes shouldn't.
First it ate old Grandmama
(Most other fishes wouldn't.

Next it ate the postman,
Third the family cat,
Then it ate our neighbour -
Just left her flowery hat!

My fish is very naughty,
It eats all it can see.
I keep well away from it,
It might just turn on me!

Peter Doubtfire (12)
St Benedict's RC High School, Alcester

AN UNEXPECTED DEATH!

Freedom, bring me freedom,
As I quiver, as I cry.
Freedom, bring me freedom,
I'm too young to die!

Honesty, bring me honesty,
Tell me what's inside.
Honesty, bring me honesty,
I'm too young to die!

Forgiveness, bring me forgiveness,
I'm sorry, sorry I sigh!
Forgiveness, bring me forgiveness,
I'm too young to die!

Time, bring me time,
I know it's almost nigh.
Time, bring me time,
I'm too young to die!

So Grandma,
Oh Grandma
. . . don't make me eat your pie!

Alenka Lamare (13)
St Benedict's RC High School, Alcester

MILLENNIUM BOOGIE

Let's leave the past behind us
The future's on its way.
Let's have a millennium party
And boogie down all day!

The springtime is here
It's time for the lambs to play.
The baby rabbits come out
And we boogie down all day.

The summer months are here
The sun is blazing down.
And all around the park
People are boogying down.

The autumn time is here
The leaves are falling down.
With all these lovely colours,
It's time to boogie down.

The winter months are here
We're chucking snowballs around.
The millennium is here
So let's *boogie on down!*

Helen Flynn (12)
St Benedict's RC High School, Alcester

WAITING

Waiting for the bell to go
How I really want it so.
Just one minute to go
How I really want it so.
Finally the bell goes
We've all got lunch now,
Got to get in the queue
Got to have some food.
Haven't eaten all day
Got to go and pay,
So I can go and play.
The bell has gone,
What a shame!
Back to lessons, no more play,
Tomorrow is another day,
So let's wait to play.

Roberto Frascona (12)
St Benedict's RC High School, Alcester

I KNOW A PLACE

I know a place where the grass shines and glows,
Where the shiny river's current gently flows,
And the flittering fairies fly,
Through the bright terracotta sky,
And the magic fairy dust floats through the delicate air
While the violet poppy heads lay bare.

I know a place where luscious honeysuckle grows,
And the amazing agrimony floats,
Through the delicate silvery thread,
I can see a fairy couple being wed.

Hayley Hartis (11)
Stratford-Upon-Avon High School

ABUSE

Why does he do it,
Is it just for fun?
Could it be, he gets a kick out of it,
Or is he on the run?

People say he needs attention,
What would they know?
It's not like school 'put him in detention'
It's more serious now!

What if he had a better life,
Would he be the same?
Maybe next time he'll use a knife,
Or end this stupid game.

I wish he would give in,
To realise his mistake.
I know he wants to, deep within,
I hope for everyone's sake.

Why doesn't he listen
To what friends are saying?
In his eyes, there is a glisten,
But everyone is paying.

Please come to reason,
To see what you are doing.
Why this, why treason,
Do you know where you're going?

Ceri Slade (15)
Stratford-Upon-Avon High School

BASKETBALL

Basketball has five players in each team.
The running sweat makes the players smelly.
Champion is my one and only dream,
The sweat smells like a farmer's wellie.

But who care? Basketball is a cool game,
The game makes the players shine like the sun.
The players in the game make their own fame,
Playing the game is their one way of fun.

I love the fast, quick sport so very, very much,
I would play it every day of the week.
The ball is so fast it is hard to touch,
They are millionaires at their finest peak.

I love the sport as much as the month of May,
The 'world champion' I shall be one day.

Peter Middleton (15)
Stratford-Upon-Avon High School

NOISE I CAN'T HEAR

Everyone is shouting loudly.
So loudly, I can't hear a word.
With so many people,
And so many opinions.
If everyone spoke,
Instead of screaming,
Maybe I could understand.
I wish I could understand.

Nicola Sach (16)
Stratford-Upon-Avon High School

Death

So many times I have thought about death,
Not scared for me but for others.
So many times I wonder where you go,
What it feels like, what it looks like.
I have never really understood death,
People die and disappear
But why and where?
Why are they taken away?
Where are they taken to?
Why are we left behind
To grieve for them and cry?
Are we being punished
For something we've done wrong?
Are we being taught a lesson
But for what reason and why?
The only thing I have learnt
Is to enjoy your every minute.
To spend time with those you care for
And to grab your every chance.
Don't spend time pondering where or why
Just let it go, because you will eventually know.

Laura Cox (14)
Stratford-Upon-Avon High School

Chat Rooms

It's the buzz you see,
Not knowing who you're talking to.
Waiting, waiting, yes! You've got a private message
Who is it going to be? Where do they come from?
America, England or even, Italy?
It's all a mystery.

Here we go, we know each other's names
Oh no, they've got to go!
Who cares there's plenty more rooms
Kenny's Cafe and Shoutouts too
It's all part of the fun.

It's what I call the mystery game.

Sarah Hicks (14)
Stratford-Upon-Avon High School

RED

What is red?
A colour, a warning,
A shepherd's delight?
The colour of love
On a hot summer's night?
A violent rage
A reminder of Christmas?
Happy days . . .
The heart is red,
It pumps out the blood.
That causes the body
With red, to flood.
From a bull's favourite colour,
To a teacher's marking pen.
Red is the colour you'll see on a hen.
Red is the colour I have on my brain.
You'd think that one day it would drive me insane!
But nevertheless, I love to see red,
At morning, in daylight and before I go to bed!
Red!

Carly Hanks (14)
Stratford-Upon-Avon High School

CA'BOOM

Tick-tock, tick-tock,
Most of the world is coming to a stop!
Rushing, hustling, wondering what to do next.
The clock is ticking, only one minute left.

Tick-tock, tick-tock,
It's almost the end of the world
As I look around, I see more and more people crying.
It is the end of life.
The world is now dying.
Clusters of people dashing to and fro
We're losing time, only twenty seconds to go.

Tick-tock, tick-tock,
Wind, rain, thunder and lightning.
10, 9, it's getting more frightening.
Bye, bye landscape, bye, bye sun and moon.
The end of humanity.
3, 2, 1, ca'boom!

Louise Welsh (15)
Stratford-Upon-Avon High School

LAS VEGAS

Las Vegas is the land of bright flashing lights,
Non-stop entertainment every day and every night.
Colourful casinos to lose all your money in.
Play blackjack, or give the roulette a spin!
Take a chance on the tables, fritter your dollars away,
But remember that gambling doesn't always pay.

Wall to wall slot machines everywhere.
All you can do is just gaze and stare.
The crashing sound of coins being won
From lines of people playing the slots for fun.

Hotels full of exhilarating rides.
Hundreds of chapels filled with blushing brides!
It's the only place that's ritzy and glitzy but also tacky!
The fun doesn't stop it's ultra-wacky!

This place exists in a desert, now I find that hard to believe.
Once you have been to Las Vegas, you won't want to leave.
Themed hotels with pyramids, a volcano, a circus and even more.
Staying in Las Vegas is anything but a bore!

Sophie Parslow (14)
Stratford-Upon-Avon High School

MY STAR

Do you see that star in the sky?
The one that is so high,
The one that shines so bright.
That star is special,
That star is kind,
A star like that - you will never find.

That is my star,
He belongs to me.
I will always love him
However far away he may be.

I wish upon him every night,
He dries the tear in my eye,
And stops me feeling sad and blue,
As I know he's watching over me too.

Lily Anstey (14)
Stratford-Upon-Avon High School

LISTEN TO ME!

Only opinions, it's not the whole story.

Wear the badge
Do you know what you're doing?
Have you listened to what he said?

His side,
He's made up his mind.
Will not listen,
Let me voice an opinion,
It's not valid.

His opinion, it's not the whole story.

Ghastly imagery,
Shock.
You demean us,
For standing up for our rights.
We are strong, I am strong.

Only opinions, it's not the whole story.

Ella Selwood (17)
Stratford-Upon-Avon High School

A SHORT POEM ABOUT MY SISTER

I have a sister of seven years old,
Mum and Dad think she is made of gold.
She comes in my bedroom and messes it up,
And I am always left to tidy it!

She is mad about horses and Beanies too,
She has got so many I don't know what to do!
With big, green eyes and curly brown hair,
I turn around and she is always there!

Even though sometimes she can be a pest,
I still think that she is the absolute best!
And that is all, I ought to be going.
This is the end of my short little poem!

Lee Stewart Coldicott (15)
Stratford-Upon-Avon High School

FUTURE LIES

As soon as the curtains opened and she went in
She could no longer hear the outside din,
Inside it was dark and dusty,
And smelt really very musty.
The fortune teller waited for her fee
Sara paid and turned with a plea,
'My exam results come in a week or so,
And if possible I want to know
What they are in advance please.'
The woman now sitting on her knees,
Looked into her crystal ball,
'In my crystal ball I see that you'll
Fail your exams. Yes! Fail them all.'
For a moment in shock Sara stared at the wall,
Then she jumped up and left in a hurry,
All of that next week, she did worry,
Until the postman came . . .
On the envelope she saw her name.
She fumbled around with the important letter,
When she saw the results, she felt much better.
But where she thought were F's and G's
Were instead . . . A's and B's.

Hazel Ingram (14)
Stratford-Upon-Avon High School

My Dearest Wish

My dearest wish -
To pass from darkness into light,
Away from where the monsters lurk,
Their forms coiling around my heart,
Like springs come alive.

My heart's desire -
To leave this dirt and all this noise,
And never point my gun or kill a man.
To walk amongst roses under a clear blue sky,
And mankind is at peace.

My deepest regret -
My scream, joining one voice,
Made up of a billion screams,
Yet still unheard, after all,
There is no profit in peace.

Jessica Eastgate (16)
Stratford-Upon-Avon High School

I Miss . . .

Her jet-black hair,
Her big brown eyes
Which told me she was so pleased to see me.
The way she came up to me and greeted me with great style.

She would lie in the chair and sleep away,
With no problems on her mind.
Sometimes I would just sit and stare and admire.

The way she jumped up at me
And gave me a great big kiss.
The way she protected me is what
I really miss.

But now these are all memories,
Just thoughts in my head.
Taken from me which I can never forget,
Our beautiful dog, Ellie!

Amber Compton (14)
Stratford-Upon-Avon High School

UNTITLED

It frustrates me,
When people misjudge,
Distort and warp facts,
Undervalue feelings.
And suppose that they understand.

It exasperates me,
When people are stubborn,
Obstinate and tenacious,
Recalcitrant and pertinacious.
And suppose that they understand.

It disconcerts me,
When people are inflexible,
Unfair and unjust,
Oppressive in their opinions,
And suppose that they understand.

Nicola Sach (16)
Stratford-Upon-Avon High School

A Question I Need To Ask

When I first saw you I knew that you were the one for me.
We met when I was talking to one of your friends.
Whenever I saw you, my stomach turned over and over and
my cheeks went slightly rosy.
I thought about you day and night.
You were the star that guided me and my strength when
I was weak.
Everything seemed too good to be true,
Just like a dream.
Until it ended, I had to go home and leave you.
Now we are separated.
I'll keep the memories of you and me inside,
and hopefully one day we will meet again.
The one thing I need to know
Is did you feel the same way?

Sarah Morris (14)
Stratford-Upon-Avon High School

It's All The Same!

Exasperated and infuriated
Why should we all be the same?
Each of us should be:
Distinctive and imperial
What's happened to the integrity?
We've lost the opportunity
To show that we can be unique
Open-minded, calm and free
The way we see ourselves to be
Why can't we be . . .
Unique?

Claire Hampstead (16)
Stratford-Upon-Avon High School

CHRISTMAS

Christmas is a special time of the year
It happens once which is very dear.
It brings excitement fun and laughter
With happiness it brings love and joy.
Which is always followed by sweet memories.

There will be decorations hanging in the streets
With angels, bells and robins.
There will be colours shining bright
With the streets full of lights.

The sound of Christmas approaches
Filling you up with that special something.
The young, old and elderly are all enjoying themselves.
Carols can be heard from every house.
It seems to know what Christmas is all about
It makes you smile and want to give.

Seeing children receive presents in such glee
You wonder how strong the feeling can be.

The sight of Christmas with the snow
Like a sheet of white silk, it sits unfolded.
When the land is covered in this snow
Everything seems to glow.

Sandy Chan (14)
Stratford-Upon-Avon High School

TUNISIAN EXPERIENCE

Waiting, waiting, waiting
Wishing time would pass more quickly.
Twenty suitcases, twenty bags
I wonder if our clothes will last?

The plane takes off
The pilot speaks.
A bumpy landing it makes me sick.
The air is hot, the smell is strong.

We wake up early onto the beach,
Into my bikini, lay on a towel.
Hot sand burns my feet,
Jellyfish swarm the sea.

German, French, Italian, Tunisian,
Different faces, different language.
Everybody is friendly,
Music in the air.

There they are messing about,
I smile shyly.
He gives a confident wave,
Go to see him, what shall I say?

It's seven o'clock
Time for dinner.
The thought of it makes my stomach churn,
Funny vegetables, funny meat,
I think I'll stick to the water.

The day has come to say goodbye,
I wonder if I'll be back soon?
Back to plain old England,
Just another year to wait.

Lucy Selwood (14)
Stratford-Upon-Avon High School

TILL DEATH DO US PART

On a dark and dreary devilish night,
City streets shimmer from silver moonlight.
A couple lay in each others arms,
With love so true, no lie could harm.

Innocence clouded what was in store,
No barrier could have protected the door.
The brute's come in with sharpened daggers,
Beginning to beat, scratch and stab her.

The man watched in despair, wanting to cry,
But he knew in his mind, 'We're going to die'.
The woman lay dead, her blood darkened the room,
And the man knew now he couldn't escape his doom.

They charged with knives, no love in their eyes,
And he wept as the pain gashed through his side.
Tumbling through darkness, writhing in pain,
In the daylight, red stain, as to where he had lain.

Their bodies were buried side by side,
In a hope to keep their love alive.
They now rest in heaven, their love more pure,
With no more pain, or suffering to endure.

True love comes from the heart,
Remember these false words: 'Till death do us part'.

Tiffany Holman (15)
Stratford-Upon-Avon High School

Daddy

Dad, whatever is the meaning?
Such a brief word, says so much.
Peculiar habits, bizarre sleeping patterns, and even mysterious smells.
His impatient temperament frequently gets the better of him.

Sits in his space of gold,
Sipping his freshly chilled, unruffled Jack Daniel's.
Casually dozing off into slumber.
Snoring endlessly, negligent to the world,
He's contented, he's in his element.

Perfectionist. All has to be proper.
No marked walls, no stained carpets.
Dragging his finger along the window sill,
Pulling that familiar irritated expression
When a particle of dust is unveiled.

Honour and admiration are given where due,
After all - he's a component of you!

Katie Strugnell (16)
Stratford-Upon-Avon High School

Mr Nobody

'Tis he who leaves the tap running
and leaves on the TV.
He leaves the towels upon the floor
and always hides the key.
He won't put the lid on the drink
everybody blames me . . .
That's not really fair, because
      it's Mr Nobody!

Cara Morgan (11)
Stratford-Upon-Avon High School

THE HUMAN RACE

The human race is a stupid thing,
Guns and tanks without a zing,
Our purpose is one single mission,
The destruction of life, for evolution,
Kill off animals and chop down trees,
Clear the land and pollute the seas,
We're selfish, racist, destructive and slow,
When we'll catch on I don't know,
Our ancestors, the primates are smart,
And I for one know full well we aren't,
We think our race is top,
But it's not,
The computer, our creation is smarter than us,
Teach it to talk, walk, drive a bus,
It's knowledge capacity bigger than mine,
Could it be, is it a sign,
Humans will shrivel, humans will die,
Computers will learn to laugh and cry.
'Bye my creator, goodbye you fool,
Didn't you realise that I could be cruel.'
They will lead the dawn of the next age,
Leftover humans will become their slaves,
But now go back to our ancestors, the primates,
And think about the lives of the apes,
Not destructive, they were just there,
Didn't care how or why or where,
But back we come to here and now,
Live another day, kill another cow,
And once again the human race,
I'll tell you now it isn't ace.

James Breen (14)
Stratford-Upon-Avon High School

SPIDERS

The eyes that twinkle
The claws that twitch
The legs of so many
It makes me itch.

They hide in corners
They live in your shoe
They'll never leave you alone
They're all after you.

They only come out at night
To spin their webs
They come out to scare you
With all eight of their legs.

You're lying awake
You're looking at the ceiling
You're scared and alert
You've got this eerie feeling!

Sarah Scowcroft (14)
Stratford-Upon-Avon High School

AT THE BEACH

The soft golden sand
That runs through my hand.
The sandcastles stand
They look so grand.

The sea is so clear
And the foghorns you can hear.
The small waves ripple up
Onto the beach
And the huge waves hit the rocks
. . . *out of my reach!*

Caroline Maisey (11)
Stratford-Upon-Avon High School

THE BLACKEST OF HEARTS

As lonely as the sky at night
A foreign country full of hate:
You're quick to judge by my dark skin
And cast me out, destroy my pride.

Discrimination, segregation, hate;
The looks, the names, tearing through my bleeding heart,
And murdering every meaning to life.
My efforts for peace are fatigued, sore, aching,

Does my goodwill deserve such torture?
Do I not feel love like you do?
Do I not feel pain or hurt or sorrow like you do?
And do I not bleed like you do, or cry tears like you do?

You're blinded by your own ignorance.
You are too stubborn to realise
That the colour of my skin does not change who I am;
So open your eyes, see the person inside.

Emma Johnson (16)
Stratford-Upon-Avon High School

DESPAIR

Lonely,
Confused,
Lost in a world that is crumbling around me.

I walk alone
For the happy faces show nothing now but overwhelming
Sadness.

Claws protrude from my fingertips,
Reaching out and piercing the bitterness in the atmosphere.

Silence.
For words can no longer express
The hatred and remorse.

Tears cascading from my eyes,
Like an ancient waterfall,
Drowning and choking in a whirlpool of emotions.

Myself an atom in despair,
Desperate to regain some family love.

Scared,
My disguise of strength and might.
Inside I am weak,
Twisted and tangled.
A young child weeping,
All alone in the world.

Hannah Ulyatt (15)
Stratford-Upon-Avon High School

PREJUDICE

The judgement, the jokes.
The horror, the hate;
The resentment, the revulsion,
The intolerance, the insults.
Prejudice: fundamentally wrong.

Unjust, unfair.
Obstinate, offensive
Patronising, prejudging
Exasperation, extreme
Discrimination, fundamentally wrong.

Live his life, feel his pain.

The frustration, the fear.
The desperation, the dread.
The hopelessness, the hurt.
The existence: the end.
You don't understand!

Angry, ashamed.
Lost, loganimity
Questions, questions
Guilt, guidance.
Feelings, forever.
You don't understand!

It can't be right; it must be wrong.

Kerry Oakes (17)
Stratford-Upon-Avon High School

MY LITTLE INVISIBLE FRIEND

I have a friend called Bee,
He is invisible to see.
When the lights go out and it is dark outside,
I know Bee is with me.

Busy Bee, invisible man,
Brown all over with his lovely tan.
Slaps on cream all over his head,
But he still manages to toast like bread!

I have a friend called Bee,
He is invisible to see.
When the lights go out and it is dark outside,
I know Bee is with me.

Down on the beach with my friend Bee,
Throwing pebbles into the sea.
Buckets and spades on the sand,
Ice-cream cornets by the band.

I have a friend called Bee,
He is invisible to see.
When the lights go out and it is dark outside,
I know Bee is with me.

Daniel Simpson (14)
Stratford-Upon-Avon High School

MAYBE

Basking in the glory of being different.
For one so unnatural, you put up a good act.
Everyone quivers, how to react?
A secret club where I'll never be accepted.
A cult, where *you* learn to be offended.

Attention and sickness: I fear
Open mind clear.
And though he laughs, we all know
It's not difficult to be indifferent.
I socialise in all the right circles.
I've spoken to many.
Why should I pay?
Attention: the only curable way.

A grey cloud hangs over my head.
A thought of nature, then turn away.
Let me know Elephant Man
Look in the mirror: ask 'Who I am'
Why do we look? Why stare?
Why do you think? You unnatural heir
To my country, the place where I live,
Turn, my mind's like a sieve.
Remind me what the truth is.
Remove the mask,
Prove it!

Simon McCoy (17)
Stratford-Upon-Avon High School

ANTHEM FOR A GEEKY YOUTH

Three years ago you may have been Top Dog
You exerted your strength on those weaker
Those with few friends
Those with low self-confidence

Three years from then and you are nothing.
A four-year cigarette habit since you were twelve
Has prevented you from growing taller than 5ft 5ins
You are a scrounger, a loser, a fraud.

But you still think you are Top Dog.

Just because you were stronger when you were 13
Doesn't mean you still are now.

Where will you be in 30 years?
You will have nothing.
And it's your fault.

Where will the geeks be in 30 years?
They will be Bill Gates
Richard Branson
Mohammad Al Fayed

You will work for them.
They will push you around.
They will decide whether to employ you or not.

Who's got the last laugh now?

Oliver Bigland (16)
Stratford-Upon-Avon High School

DADDY

As I say this word, childhood memories drift through my mind,
The way it used to be . . .
The affection and love,
A house filled with dedication and thought.

My first bike,
Hours were spent teaching me how to ride alone.
My first bed
Restless nights spent singing me to sleep.
The feeling of success shared among us all,
as I passed my first piano exam.
Your admiration was my strength.

Your love for gardening and all things natural,
The flight of an owl,
Or the sight of a robin.
Your endless enthusiasm shone through us all.

Now . . .
You sip your woody red wine,
Smoke your bitter smelling pipe,
And refuse to communicate, as you seem to travel
through life alone.
Your shell remains the same.
Your eyes and lips have yet to change.
Your smile is seen less often,
You come and go, with the demands of work,
But as time proceeds, you seem to be slowly
slipping away from me and my memories
      as a *daddy's girl!*

Anna Turton (16)
Stratford-Upon-Avon High School

Daddy

My dad is always there for me
when he's at home.
To teach and guide and comfort me,
I never feel alone.

He takes me fishing when he can,
to catch a fish or two.
He seems to be a model man,
is there nothing he can't do?

He works all day and then at night
he sits down in his chair.
His dirty clothes, he is a sight,
he needs to cut his hair.

Even so he tries his best,
he's happy all the same.
I know sometimes, I am a test,
he keeps his cool - he's tame.

His temperament is sometimes cruel,
sometimes bitter, sometimes mad.
This happens when I disobey him,
but underneath there still lies respect.

He is my dad, I won't deny
he takes value in my interests.
I show him proudly, I know no shame,
come see people . . . he's my daddy.

Stuart Taylor (16)
Stratford-Upon-Avon High School

SNOWDROPS

Snowdrops dripping on the mountain top,
Running off the frosty, frightful mountain.
The snowdrops run off the clouds
And off the rising blazing sun.
The snowdrops run off the blazing blizzard.
The snowdrops run off a shining couplet of a star
Shining down on me.
The snowdrops run off the shining moon.
Looking down on me.
The snowdrops are running down on me,
And looking after me.
The snowdrops are hailing down on glittering gutter
With the ice like crystal gold, like chimes on a porch door.
The snowdrops run off my chimney roof and the birds
Cheep and chatter on my bronze patio doors.

Sarah Fernott (11)
Stratford-Upon-Avon High School

THE VOICE OF AN ANGEL

The voice of an angel
came to me in my dreams.
The sweetest, most wonderful sound.

It was carried in the breeze
and overseas
through every village and town.

Whoever's ear it may have reached,
no matter how young or old,
they would never forget the way it smiled,
the warm bright smile of an angel.

Zoë Smith (15)
Stratford-Upon-Avon High School

THE WORMS

It is me.
It is you.
It is everyone.
At times we are all it,
But all the time we are not.
These people are the worms.
The glasses,
Side partings,
Short,
Squirmy,
Plebs.
Self-centred,
Selfish,
Careless worms.
Gracious they are not.

The traffic wardens, taxmen, troublemakers.
These worms wriggle around annoying our system.
They find that part of your brain,
The part frustration or anger can only dream about.
Aggravating, irritating it beyond belief.

Just doing your job?

I do appreciate this,
I just wish you knew the full situation.
The whole scene.
It's as if you have a personal hate against me.
A grudge.

Just doing your job?

But your stereotypical look and nature!
Dressed to annoy.
To hate.
To displease.
Like a worm that enjoys tormenting *my* life.

Just doing your job?

James Righton (16)
Stratford-Upon-Avon High School

HALLOWE'EN

There it lay, left for many years in decay,
A weird eerie presence fell over the scene,
The silence was rich and overpowering.
Could this be the worst scene in history?

The grotesque, deteriorating features lay over the body,
Like a plague had devoured some skin and muscle.
The sneering head looked at me,
Waiting for me to creep closer
I resisted . . . the temptation was easy to overcome.

Suddenly it moved
The rotting arm rose from the dugout grave.
Carrion peeled off the arm, like the skin from cold custard.
I screamed, the echo blasted into the depths of the forest.
I ran for my life into unknown lands.

I found myself at home, early - in the waking hours.
I was terrified.
My friend met me later that morning
I don't know why, as he vanished before we got to the forest.
Then he said 'Did you have a happy Hallowe'en?'

Marcus Lemberger (14)
Stratford-Upon-Avon High School

A Furry Lion Mask And A Cardboard Sailing Boat

Steam train rides with him, passing rows of trees,
green, green fields and waving farmer's crops.
Sitting on the giant brown leather sofa in front of him
while a frothy lather was made all over my arms and legs.
Glorious flowers planted in the garden by him,
creating an ocean of colour.
The scolding of my brother by him, after splashing me
in the polka dot paddling pool.
The colour blue.
The colour of the shoes worn by him on holiday
in Western Super Mare.
A furry lion mask, and a cardboard sailing boat made with him,
for the peculiar tasks set at school.
The numerous stripy, spotty and chequered ties owned by him,
one for each day of the week.
Eating lime green jelly made by him, whilst sitting
on the orange and yellow magic carpet.
Playing with the top button of the pinky-white shirt worn by him,
and squashing his legs with my wriggly bottom in the process.
Never being punished by him, for doing things I oughtn't,
even after pinching my sister's arm 'till it was almost purple.
Being hoisted up in the air by him at Bourton-on-the-Water,
so that I could see the penguins.
Walking down the gravely path with him, clutching his hand
and tugging his arm down so low that it was nearer his knees
than his waist.
All taken away . . . all gone!
But my memories still remain.

Anna Sanders (16)
Stratford-Upon-Avon High School

TICK-TOCK

Tick-tock went the clock
The hands of time are turning.
Tick-tock went the clock
The future I behold.

Tock-tick went the clock
For I have seen the future.
Tock-tick went the clock
The future I will tell.

Tick-tock went the clock
The voices I have heard.
Tick-tock went the clock
The voices of the world.

Tock-tick went the clock
The future it is clear.
Tock-tick went the clock
The future's full of fate.

Tick-tock went the clock
The trees they do not flourish.
Tick-tock went the clock,
Nature she is dead.

Tock-tick went the clock,
For the future becomes present.
Tock-tick went the clock
Time drawing to an end.

Tick-tock went the clock
I am the voice of future.
Tick-tock went the clock.
Tick-tock!

Lisa Fernandes (14)
Stratford-Upon-Avon High School

Daddy And My Father

Daddy is a figure from the past,
My father; he is now.

Daddy is a figure from childhood,
so huge, invincible and tall.
He overshadows my world like a mountain,
raising me when I fall.

Daddy is the crinkling newspaper on Sunday.
The wet weekend, the joint of lamb.
Daddy is the suit at the breakfast table,
Always the tie - the businessman.

Daddy is the doorbell chiming at night,
a dream as I drift towards sleep.
Daddy is the other duvet mound,
when into my parent's room I creep.

My father may not be invincible,
and I no longer his greatest fan.
But when the day is over, I know
he was Daddy . . . that very same man.

Daddy is a figure from the past,
My father; he is now.

Tom Fidler (16)
Stratford-Upon-Avon High School

DADDY

The doorbell rings, it's 6 o'clock
I run to the door, excitement building up inside
I reach to open the door and there you are
The magical smile that could only belong to you
You pick me up and spin me round and round
I grab on to you tight, scared to let go

The chair in the lounge looked empty without you
The misty green colour, the tea stain on the arm rest, from Christmas
Your glasses rested on the coffee table nearby
Which you were always losing
Your slippers placed next to your chair, like marking your territory
The half-read newspaper folded down the side of the chair

The summer days spent in the garden, playing football with you
We made the goals from flower pots
Which would always end up being damaged
You would always show off and say you were better
But I'd take no notice
That green Ireland shirt you always used to wear
That was too small for you, but you didn't care

Memories are precious and should never be lost
My memories of my daddy will never be lost - ever!

Rebecca Caden (16)
Stratford-Upon-Avon High School

Perfect Day

There are no boundaries anymore
No restrictions.
A misting magic golden sky
an umbrella of pure paradise, colours,
floating above a flowing glass ocean.
Surroundings which make everything important
fade and only leave *the perfect day*.
Nature has broken all its laws, replacing them
with an unmeasurable element of surprise.
Almost as if your perfection has pleased the world
and it feels it must flatter and praise you.
Floating on a stretch of crystal satin water
as if on a cloud.
Now I feel as though I have been given
a precious gift.
Fragile and perfect.
To see these subtle, tender colours,
never seen before.
As if standing high on a bird's wing,
feathers spread and regal.
You and the day are equal and harmonious.
At peace with all and each other.
We don't need to speak
we both know each others thoughts
pure contentment . . .
We will sail to the world's end
you will row thoughtful and content.
I will trail my hand in the warm,
cut glass water.
A picture of perfection,
that is how it will stay
forever . . .

Keira Wilson (14)
Stratford-Upon-Avon High School

The Scream

I stand high upon the bridge
Above the murky lake
The river goes on running by
I'm trapped, I can't escape.

I'm all alone
There's no one there
The passers-by
Seem not to care.

I'm scared
But no one can understand
I can't break free
From this nightmare land

The blood-red sky
The sunset's low
A swirling mess
The wind a-blow

My life has gone
My love has left
I can hear nothing more
Than the call for death!

Rebecca Young (14)
Stratford-Upon-Avon High School

Daddy

Daddy, all dressed in blue
Looking for an adventure.
But no sense of direction,
We're lost again in the mountains.

Perfection.
Everything must be right.
No bending the rules
Everyone must meet your standards.

A figure of calmness.
Won't show your feelings.
Have to be strong
Why won't you tell us when you're hurt?

Protection.
Try to hold on.
Don't want us to grow up
Too much love perhaps.
Try to protect us from the world.

Unconditional love.
Whatever we may do,
Though we may disagree
I'll always love you too.

Grace McAteer (16)
Stratford-Upon-Avon High School